We dedicate this book to our respective children, and the many youth and young adults who have made us better people, pastors, and leaders, and given us a beautiful vision for what the church can and should be!

May we continue learning from you.

Followers Under 40 by Rachel Gilmore and Kris Sledge is a pastoral gift for the church at this critical moment. With deep wisdom, lived experience, and relevant research, they speak to the urgent challenges facing older congregations while casting a vision for the kind of ministry that can reach the distinct generational proclivities of Millennials, Gen Z, and Gen Alpha. If your congregation is willing to change to minister well to younger generations, then read and discuss this book together with your worshipping community.

Rev. Dr. Drew Hart
Associate Professor of Theology at Messiah University
Author of *Who Will Be A Witness?: Igniting Activism for God's Justice, Love, and Deliverance*

This book is an invaluable gift to the church, as simple as that. In a season where congregations must find ways to engage younger people with the Gospel, this book provides a practical hope to accomplish that biblical mandate. And the best part is that it's a book not designed for church growth or self-service but to genuinely love younger people the Jesus way. Every church leader needs to read this book.

Rev. Dr. Rodrigo Cruz
Executive Assistant to the Bishop
North & South Georgia Conferences of the United Methodist Church

Followers Under Forty: The Journey Away from Church in the Age of Millennials, Gen Z, and Gen Alpha is not your typical "do this... and they will come" guide. Instead, Rachel Gilmore and Kristopher Sledge take us on a deep, transformational exploration of the values, daily lives, and spiritual longings of today's emerging generations. At a time when the church is grappling with a widening generational gap, this book offers honest insights, reflections, and practical strategies to build authentic connections and relationships with Millennials, Gen Z, and Gen Alpha. This is a must-read for pastors and church leaders eager to partner with God in making Christ's healing and liberating love real and relevant to younger generations.

Bishop Héctor A. Burgos-Núñez
Susquehanna Conference & Upper New York Area of The United Methodist Church

Kris and Rachel have crafted a powerful and essential guide in *Followers Under 40*, addressing the pressing disconnect between the church and younger generations. Through their deep understanding of Millennials, Gen Z, and Gen Alpha, they illuminate the challenges and opportunities facing faith communities today. Their personal experiences as church planters and innovators bring authenticity and urgency to the conversation.

This book is not just a critique of the current state of the church; it is a call to action. Kris and Rachel offer insightful analysis and practical strategies aimed at fostering genuine engagement with young adults. Their vision for creating inclusive, diverse, and vibrant faith communities resonates deeply at a time when many feel alienated from organized religion.

What sets *Followers Under 40* apart is its hopeful outlook and commitment to envisioning a more relevant church for future generations. The authors invite readers to reflect on their own contexts while providing a roadmap for rebuilding trust and integrity within the church. With its honest exploration of the barriers young adults face, this book serves as both a mirror and a guide for church leaders, pastors, and congregants alike.

In a landscape where many are leaving the church, Kris and Rachel remind us of the profound potential for transformation that lies within. *Followers Under 40* is a must-read for anyone passionate about revitalizing the church and ensuring it remains a vital instrument for good, healing, and justice in the world.

Michael Adam Beck
Director of Fresh Expressions for The United Methodist Church.
Author, *Never Alone: Sharing the Gift of Community in a Lonely World*

Gilmore and Sledge have written a gem. *Followers Under 40* blends compassionate truth-telling with the practical wisdom of two pastors who have spent their careers building congregations alongside young adults. Gilmore and Sledge's empathy for both congregations and young people shines through on every page, and they offer refreshingly practical guidance on how to authentically connect. But they are also bold and unflinchingly honest. Once I started reading, I couldn't stop.

Kenda Creasy Dean
Princeton Theological Seminary
Author, *Innovating for Love and Almost Christian: What the Faith of Our Teenagers Is Telling the American Church*

I read this book from bifocal lenses: as a parent of two Gen Z kids who continue to discern their place in the church (or if there is any place for them at all) and as judicatory leader of a denomination that continues to wrestle with what it means to welcome young people. Rachel and Kris are ministry practitioners who offer us insights that will help us understand these generations we are trying to reach and layout a trail map of practical ways to ensure that we don't fashion these young people into our own image but allow them to discover and live into the image of God that is already in them! I commend this book to everyone who genuinely seeks to be in authentic relationship with young people in their communities of faith.

Bishop Carlo A. Rapanut
Desert Southwest Conference & New Mexico Conference of The United Methodist Church

Rachel Gilmore and Kris Sledge offer an unflinchingly honest assessment of the current state of the church: aging buildings, aging congregants, aging clergy, and declining membership. But this is not a book that wallows in despair at what once was! Together, they provide insights into emerging generations and practical ways churches can revise ministries to provide pathways for intergenerational communities where faith intersects with life in transforming ways.

Bishop Karen Oliveto
Retired Bishop of The United Methodist Church

FOLLOWERS
UNDER 40

The journey away from church for Millennials, Gen Z, and Gen Alpha

Rachel Gilmore & Kris Sledge

FOLLOWERS UNDER 40

The journey away from church for Millennials, Gen Z, and Gen Alpha

©2025 Market Square Publishing, LLC

books@marketsquarebooks.com
141 N. Martinwood, Suite 2 • Knoxville, Tennessee 37923

ISBN: 978-1-950899-89-0

Printed and Bound in the United States of America
Cover Illustration & Book Design ©2025 Market Square Publishing, LLC

Editor: Sheri Carder Hood
Cover Design: Kevin Slimp
Page Design: Carrie Rood
Post Production Editor: Ken Rochelle

Scripture quotations used with permission from:

Scripture quotations marked (NIV) are taken from the Holy Bible,
New International Version®, NIV®. Copyright © 1973, 1978, 1984, 2011 by Biblica, Inc.®
Used by permission of Zondervan. All rights reserved worldwide.
www.zondervan.com The "NIV" and "New International Version" are trademarks
registered in the United States Patent and Trademark Office by Biblica, Inc.®

Contents

FOREWORD

Followers Under 40

I can't complete a workshop, conference address, or denominational meeting without being asked that one fateful question: *"So how can we get young people into the church?"*

This book is just about the most direct, concise response to that question that I have found. But rather than the usual litany of tactics ("fix your lighting," "update your fonts"), *Followers Under 40* creates a pathway of empathy to Millennials, Gen Z, and Gen Alpha. It's not just about recruitment; it's about relationship.

The "followers" they're talking about here, by the way, are followers of Jesus. The goal isn't "followers of the pastor," "followers of the denomination," or even "followers of the church." Indeed, the three generations in question can see through that from a mile away (or a Google away). Indeed, as trust for any institution—the school system, the Supreme Court, even the post office—erodes, it's important that our work is transparently about cultivating faith in God, not allegiance to institutions.

And yet, the church is nonetheless essential for God's work in the world. As a pastor, I know a certain type of transformation can only happen within the church and that gathering people to share the Good News of God will never be outsourced to AI. God made us to practice spirituality in community, and church is certainly *my* favorite place for that to happen!

I'm grateful for the way Gen Z and Gen Alpha relate to the church in the same way that I'm grateful for how moving apartments forces me to get rid of things. When you're boxing everything up to move across town, you have to pause and ask: *do I REALLY need this broken couch?*

And, likewise, Gen Z is forcing us to ask: *Do we REALLY need to meet in a building? Does it REALLY need to be synchronous? Does it REALLY need to use the lectionary?*

The answer might be yes! But, similar to when we're switching apartments, the question forces us to hold on to what is *actually* most important to us, and that is always a worthwhile activity.

Further, the American church has some deeper questions to address: *Do we REALLY need to collude with white supremacy culture to garner a following? Do we REALLY need to sit idly by as unbridled capitalism objectifies our neighborhood? Do we REALLY need to pretend "all are welcome" while our states continue to brutalize transgender young people?*

And so forth. (Rachel and Kris make an excellent case for the response to that question, by the way, so keep reading). Just like the prophets of the Bible, Millennials, Gen Z, and Gen Alpha are calling their societies and faith communities to change, and it's the church's opportunity to follow, even if the path is not entirely clear.

My prayer is that this book leads you into relationship, not recruitment. If you've ever met Rachel or Kris, you know they are some of the most relationship-oriented people who have walked this earth since Jesus. Soak in how they approach these three generations (including if you are in one of them, like me), and let it provoke you to establish generational bridges in every direction.

Rev. Tyler Sit

Author, Pastor, and Co-Founder of Intersect: a Co-Planting Network

Introduction to Epistles

Letters to the Generations

Most of our New Testament exists today because Paul wrote letters to churches he visited and started throughout the Mediterranean. Now, we do not claim to be like the Apostle Paul, but we wondered what Paul might say to our churches and communities in the 21st century. Those letters might look something like this:

Dear Aging Congregations:

We see you. We see your years of faithfulness, the decades spent teaching Sunday School, singing in the choir, serving in church leadership, and giving so generously of your time, talents, and resources. We see the offerings of the "builder" generation, literally thousands of churches and steeples that you helped to construct with your own hearts and hands as you dreamed of future generations. We see how frightened you were by COVID when the world shut down, and you felt so isolated and alone. You missed your church family and waited for the day when you could gather again and sing boldly, unmasked, before God and each other.

Church changed a lot when you had to move to online worship or socially distanced outdoor seating. We saw the longing in your eyes to go back to the way things were, back to the good old days when going to church on Sundays was a guiding principle and priority in the life of the community.

And now, as you look around your sanctuary, you see empty seats. You see gray hair, lower energy, and slower movement. You still work, teach, sing, serve, and give faithfully. You do everything you did before but wonder, at times, for whose good? Where is the next generation? Where are the young families? "If only we had young people," you cry out, "we wouldn't be in this place." Where is the future of the church? And you try not to take it personally. "Times have changed," they say. "We are spiritual but not religious." Maybe everything shouldn't change with time. What if you can be spiritual AND religious and show up to church with your grandma every once in a while?

You hear what the younger people are saying, but it doesn't take away your pain, the deep heartache, and the growing emptiness inside. The confusion and the anger and, yes, the fear. Because what if you gave your whole life to a church that won't even be open long enough to host your funeral? What if the "faith of our fathers" that you taught to your kids and grandkids seems to be a forgotten tale in a world you don't recognize anymore? Maybe you tried adding a drum set to the sanctuary or hired a children's minister, but no matter what you do, they aren't showing up on Sundays. How can the church change so much in one's lifetime?

So you sigh, you pray, and you hope with all that you have left that there is an answer you haven't yet explored. You hope that those you love will know the love of God— and that the church, which has played such a central role in your life, will continue to mean something to those who come after you. You keep singing and serving and showing up because you don't know what else to do. Those faithful acts keep you grounded and bring you peace in these most uncertain times. We see you. We hear you. You are not alone.

Dear Millennials, Generation Z, and Generation Alpha:

We see you. The church and religious landscape you are inheriting and experiencing is a challenge. The faith and religion of your parents or grandparents has largely left you wanting more, wanting something deeper, and wondering if it is relevant and necessary to your life. And honestly, you're right. Your feelings and thoughts about the church, organized religion, and faith are real and honest.

Over the past decade and more, you have heard about significant scandals and news stories highlighting the fracturing of the Christian church. You have read horrifying stories of church scandals, misuse of power by religious leaders, pastors with little integrity, spiritual trauma, and significant division in denominational groups. For some, these stories have been about you. Or, they have been about your friends. Perhaps they simply have left you wondering about the integrity, purpose, and role of religion and the church today. Before we spend an entire book talking about the good, bad, and ugly of followers under 40 today and how the church and leaders can be more faithful in their leadership with the emerging generations, we want to apologize to you.

To our Millennial, Generation Z, and Generation Alpha siblings, we lament with you on what is left. We are sorry for the poor examples of leadership, faith, and Jesus you have witnessed and now must sift through to wrestle with your own relationship with the divine and the church. In our failure, we have alienated and harmed you, particularly and grievously our LGBTQIA+ and Black, Indigenous, and people of color (BIPOC) siblings. In many ways, the church has become known for its hate-filled rhetoric, oppressive theological convictions, and non-life-giving practices. The church has often been known for who and what it is against and not known for love.

So, we understand why you may not trust religious leaders. Why you may have chosen to leave the church and struggle to hold on to your faith in God makes sense. The church has been messy and harmful. We see you. We see the pain we've caused, and we want to seek your forgiveness.

And yet, amid the messiness and harm, the truth is that there is no future without you. And we don't mean that in a weird, "come to church so we can keep the doors open" kind of way. What we mean is that we believe the church is where transformation happens, an important transformation that is not replicated anywhere else in society, and if you do not participate in that transformation, then our future is a spiritually weakened one. We need your prophetic witness to re-imagine how churches, pastors, and denominational leaders can once again be a people of peace, justice, and healing in the world. We pray that this book adequately gives voice to the significant harm done by and in the church, and yet, we imagine a new day where the specific voices of the emerging generations lead us into a future marked by beauty and hope.

SETTING THE STAGE

Creating Space for the Next Generation

Kris (he/him) and Rachel (she/her) first met when Rachel was recruiting Kris to join the staff of her thriving church plant in Virginia Beach, Virginia. What began as a friendly recruiting call became a decade-long friendship and collegial relationship. Kris declined Rachel's invitation, not once, but twice, to join her church plan while he launched a new church community in Harrisburg, Pennsylvania. Separated by a decade in age but both Millennials, Kris and Rachel are innovators and church planters at heart. Interestingly, both Rachel and Kris are part of a clergy couple, married to a pastor, respectively (Rachel married to Brandon, and Kris married to Hannah), who faithfully lead and pastor established congregations. Kris and Rachel both became parents while leading new church plants and successfully planted new, growing, and diverse faith communities that reach young adults and young families. They are both equally passionate about living out compelling, thriving new faith expressions, which led to this book.

Through many phone calls, text messages, and conversations at conferences, Kris and Rachel realized they care deeply for the Church and faith communities and want to see even more churches, pastors, and faith communities experience fruitfulness and beautiful relationships with young adults today. Some of the most influential parts of their church plants are the thriving and expanding number of young adults, young families, youth, and children who deeply engage with God and their specific church communities.

Rachel and her family moved to Phoenix a few years ago to assume a denominational role to inspire new expressions of faith in that region, and yet, her church plant continues to thrive and reach young adults today. Under Rachel's and Kris's leadership in these church plants, more than 65 percent of their active participants are under the age of forty, and they regularly see new, younger, and more diverse people engaging deeply and leading. They prioritize giving space for new, young, and diverse people to lead and engage in the church together. And now Rachel and Kris are thrilled to be co-founders with three brilliant leaders of Intersect Network (https://www.intersectnetwork.co/) who aspire to journey with innovators seeking gospel liberation in the world.

With *Followers Under 40*, Kris and Rachel hope to help others prioritize and give space to emerging generations in beautiful, profound, and unique ways and to think critically about the ways the church may not be adequately prepared. They long for more churches and pastors to have beautiful stories and sacred spaces for young adults to experience belonging, community, and God. Kris and Rachel still firmly believe that the church is one of God's best instruments to bring about good, healing, and justice in the world. But to believe in a conviction like this, we must acknowledge the significant ways the church has failed and caused harm in the world. With openness and honesty, we will share our experiences and data regarding today's young adults and

10

offer a few approaches that will hopefully help re-frame the church's integrity and effectiveness.

Followers Under 40 is our best attempt at sharing about the potential problems within the church today that make it ill-equipped to engage faithfully with young adults. This book is designed to give space for holy imagination—to explore and envision new paradigms that will allow young adults to thrive and deeply engage in the church. We are using the most updated language at the time of this publishing, but new terms will emerge as the discourse rapidly evolves. If so, we ask for grace and offer this book as a snapshot in time rather than a definitive textbook of terms.

We divided our work into three sections to stimulate our thinking and imagination. Before we get to Section One, we offer our best attempts at naming some problems the church has today. As Millennial pastors ourselves, we recognize that there are limits, liabilities, and problems. We hope to give voice to them and create space for you to name what you're experiencing in your current context.

Section One centers on who we are talking about when we use language like "young adults." We offer our best attempt at giving a brief yet compelling picture of the emerging generations and young adults today. Specifically, you will find a chapter centered on Millennials, persons born between 1980-1996, and the unique, key experiences they have experienced. We will offer a picture of Generation Z (Gen Z), persons born between 1997-2012, and how they differ from Millennials and their unique shifts and traits as an emerging generation. The last chapter in this section will center on Generation Alpha (Gen Alpha), persons born between 2012-2024. We will offer an initial picture of this generation, recognizing the unique things that will change as they reach puberty and adulthood.

After establishing a clear and working picture of these three generations, you will find a section on the three common problems and concerns they have with the church. A chapter on each generation is included to help others understand the fundamental concern young adults have with the church, as well as a compelling narrative about why these are significant barriers. Once we have a clear picture of the young adults today and understand their common concerns with the church, we offer specific ways to address these problems. These approaches will *not* solve the problems—we want to be honest and fair about this upfront—but we do think each of the five practices will decrease the concerns and rebuild trust, integrity, and effectiveness with emerging and young adults. They are a step in the right direction.

In writing *Followers Under 40,* we hope to allay your fears and inspire you to meaningfully cultivate and co-create churches that are life-giving, diverse, inclusive, and compelling with these emerging generations. As current leaders in the church today, we should critically examine ourselves to ensure we are creating space for the next generation in the church. We find ourselves with a moral imperative. As the stewards of God's church, we must do everything in our capacity and ability to foster environments that seek the healing of the church and world we inherited from previous generations.

CHAPTER ONE

Problems the Church Faces Today

Aging Congregations

Let's face it: the church is aging. A 2020 Faith Communities Today study found that 42 percent of Protestant churches have congregations where at least half the members are over sixty-five. While 17 percent of the general population of the United States is over sixty-five years old, almost half of Christians who attend church are in that age group. The same study found correlations between older pastors and the number of senior citizens in the church. Additional correlations are "being less likely to change, diminished spiritual vitality, less desire to look for new members, and to have not grown in the past five years."[1] If we broaden the definition of "older adults" to fifty and above, then 62 percent of those sitting in United Methodist pews would fit that demographic, according to a May 2024 article by *The Christian Century*.[2] The difficult reality is the church in the United States is aging quickly.

---

[1] https://research.lifeway.com/2021/11/01/americas-pastors-and-churchgoers-are-getting-older/.

[2] https://www.christiancentury.org/features/missed-opportunities-umc-general-conference#:~:text=Too percent20scary percent20to percent20mention percent20were,them percent20are percent20over percent20age percent2050.

Aging Pastors

Not only are churches aging, but the pastors are, too. The median age of a pastor is fifty-seven years old, and The United Methodist Church has seen a 32 percent decrease in the number of clergy under thirty-five years old since 2019, according to the 2022 Lewis Center Clergy Report.[3] This means that only 6 percent of clergy in the United Methodist Church are under thirty-five years old, with 41 percent falling between the ages of thirty-five and fifty-four and the remaining 53 percent being fifty-five to seventy-two years old. In a *Christianity Today* article from March of 2023, they noted that "30 years ago, 33 percent of pastors were under 40 and the median age was 44."[4] This finding is felt so clearly as we do not have many young adults eager to attend seminary. In fact, research shows that from 2003 to 2022, the seminary attendance for the top seven mainline schools dropped by 45 percent, from 11,671 students to 6,461.[5] The clergy in our churches are aging and retiring at a rate that leaves us with significant concerns, and seminary enrollment is significantly lower and not offsetting these retirements enough.

Shrinking Congregations

Our clergy are aging, our churches are aging, and our churches are shrinking in number. In June 2023, *The New York Times* reported that 40 million people have left the

---

[3] https://www.churchleadership.com/wp-content/uploads/2022/10/Clergy-Age-Trends-Report-2022.pdf.

[4] https://www.christianitytoday.com/news/2023/april/pastor-succession-church-next-generation-leader-barna-surve.html.

[5] https://www.graphsaboutreligion.com/p/seminary-education-in-2022.

church in the last twenty-five years.[6] Pew Research found
that those attending church at least once a month dropped
from 33 percent before the pandemic to 30 percent in 2022.
The decline in church attendance was felt most acutely by
Black Protestants, whose attendance went from 61 percent to
46 percent post-COVID, perhaps due to the disproportionate
number of Black Americans impacted by COVID-19 who chose
to worship online instead of in the pews.[7]

To take this one step further, our churches are also failing
to reach young adults moving into metropolitan areas. In 2020, a
large-scale national survey found that 70 percent of the estimated
350,000 to 375,000 churches in the United States had one hundred
or fewer attendees on a Sunday.[8] So, most small churches,
with large hopes for full-time staff and program budgets, do
not have critical mass for long-term sustainability. The same
national survey found that 70 percent of people who go to church
attend churches larger than 250 people, and about 75 percent
of churches are located in the north central or southern states.
Twenty-five percent of churches report being in rural areas,
with 22 percent identifying as small towns, 28 percent as large
metropolitan cities, and 25 percent in the suburbs.

These numbers seem to point to an even division of
churches until you compare them with the 2020 Census data,
which shows that 6 percent of Americans live in rural areas,

[6] https://www.nytimes.com/2023/06/21/opinion/religion-dechurching.html.

[7] (https://www.pewresearch.org/religion/2023/03/28/how-the-pandemic-has-
     affected-attendance-at-u-s-religious-services/#:~:text=This percent20longitudinal
     percent20analysis percent20finds percent20a,) percent20to percent2030 percent25
     percent20in percent202022.) https://apnews.com/article/black-protestant-church-
     attendance-youth-COVID-pandemic-5d854b4db73e118cb22767220573455f#.

[8] https://faithcommunitiestoday.org/wp-content/uploads/2021/10/Faith-
     Communities-Today-2020-Summary-Report.pdf.

8 percent in small towns, and 86 percent in metropolitan areas.[9] The reality is we have the smallest number of churches in our largest metropolitan areas. If 86 percent of Americans live in large cities and only 28 percent of our churches are located there, we are not reaching areas with the greatest concentration of people.

This past year, I (Rachel) attended the final worship service of Central United Methodist Church in Phoenix, Arizona. It was the first Protestant church in Phoenix, with a history of over 150 years, but even with tens of thousands living within walking distance of the church, they could not turn the tide of decades of decline. It was heartbreaking to attend their last worship service, but I'm hopeful that the property will be repurposed and continue to serve those in need, helping others connect to Christ through whatever new things are birthed in that space.

Leaving the Church

So, when do people stop attending church? While we may think that young adults leave church during their college years and return when they have children, that is sadly not the case. The Survey Center on American Life reported that almost 75 percent of eighteen- to twenty-nine-year-olds who leave the church decide to leave **before they are eighteen**.[10] Before a young adult leaves home to enter the adult world, they have already determined that they will or will not remain a part of a local church.

---

[9] https://faithcommunitiestoday.org/wp-content/uploads/2021/10/Faith-Communities-Today-2020-Summary-Report.pdf.

[10] https://www.americansurveycenter.org/research/generation-z-future-of-faith/.

The same survey shows that the majority of Gen Zers do not believe it is necessary to raise children in a religion, with only 40 percent indicating that it is important for children to learn morals in church. This statistic is a stark comparison to 76 percent of the Silent Generation and 68 percent of Baby Boomers who believe it is important to raise children in church.

When Did the Decline Begin?

Philip Jenkins' *Fertility and Faith* book suggests that declining birth rates are the single best indicator of declining church participation in white America, but the issue might be larger than that. One of the most significant books to be published on this issue in recent years is *The DeChurching of America*[11], which reports that, historically, we have seen three major religious shifts prior to our current reality.

The first shift was an increase in the number of Christians who joined the church in the years during and decades following the First Great Awakening. The next shift occurred during the Second Great Awakening, another season of intentional revival and spiritual growth in the United States. The third shift was an even larger increase in the number of people attending church over the decades following the Civil War as life returned to normal and communities were reshaped. However, the authors note that more people have left the church in the last twenty-five years than those who came to faith during both the First and Second Great Awakenings and everyone who converted to Christianity during the Billy Graham crusades. This shift, which began way before the outbreak of COVID-19, is unlike

---

[11] Jim Davis, Michael Graham, and Ryan P. Burge, *The Great Dechurching of America,* Zondervan, 2023.

anything our nation and church has ever experienced, and it is the first time church attendance and identification as a Christian has fallen below the majority in American history.

Why Do They Stop Attending?

While *The Great DeChurching* does not focus specifically on young adults, it does highlight three reasons why people generally stopped affiliating with Christianity beginning in the 1990s. The first reason was that, at the end of the Cold War, people no longer considered the terms *American* and *Christian* to be synonymous. During the Cold War, American media and politics tried to pit the "evil and godless Soviet Union" against the "good and Godly American" nation. Americans began to see their national identity connected to Christian spirituality. But when the Cold War ended, the culture-based faith of many Christians grew cold, and they no longer felt bound to identify themselves as Christians simply because they lived in the US.

The next general shift highlighted by *The Great DeChurching* is the rise of the Internet in the early 2000s, where people could now, for the first time, access different views on faith and religion. The Internet has led to a global movement and accessibility of faith that no longer requires someone to dress up and sit in a pew on Sunday mornings. The greater accessibility of religious practices and ideological convictions has changed the landscape and practices of Christianity in the United States.

The authors of *The Great DeChurching* note that the final shift aligns with the rise of Christian nationalism and how closely far-right fundamentalist Christians allied themselves with the Republican Party and continue to do so now. People who were, and continue to be, turned off by this radicalized faith found themselves leaving. They left not just the political party but also the church that demanded that if you follow Christ, you should vote "red." It is no surprise that the term "exvangelical" became popular in 2016 during the time of a polarizing presidential election where Christians felt pressured to vote for a particular candidate to save their faith and preserve their morals.

Why Should We Care?

We know there's a problem: people are no longer coming to church, and the church and pastors are aging. But why does this matter beyond mere institutional survivability? We are not United Methodist pastors because we want to save the structure and institution of the church. We are pastors because we feel that we have found good news that has transformed every aspect of our lives. This good news of Jesus could lead to the transformation of the world into a place of peace, equity, grace, and love for all God's children. The decline matters—and not because we need more "butts in seats" to pay our utility bills and keep the church doors open long enough for our funerals. The decline matters because the way of Jesus can bring hope and healing to those who are feeling increasingly isolated and alone.

While *The Great DeChurching* in America might list some reasons for the decline, we suggest ineffective discipleship pathways are an additional cause. We have become so accustomed to clergy doing all of the church's work that we have not effectively taught people how to truly live like Jesus and share their life of faith with those around them.

19

When we ask younger generations why they do not go to church, they share two main reasons:

- Church is not relevant to their lives.
- The people in church do not act like followers of Christ.

How many countless generations before us failed to show the relevancy of their faith in ways that made it enticing to those who came after them? How many adults have sat in adult Sunday School classes for decades yet feel ill-equipped to teach anyone else about Jesus? If we cannot shift from learning to living our faith, there is no need for an institution because there is nothing to save; there is no one who knows how to live as a follower of Jesus.

Shortly after the rise of "exvangelicals," we began hearing about the process of "deconstructing faith." This process is where Christians reflect on their faith journey and determine if the beliefs they were taught earlier in their lives are ones they still profess. While many churches are threatened by the deconstruction of faith, we find it hopeful. It means young adults are trying to think and explore faith from a more curious and critical standpoint. Faith is not something they merely subscribe to; it is a way of life, a way of discipleship. The question is, how can we engage these young adults on their journeys of deconstruction and reconstruction in the years to come? To do so, we must spend time learning the specifics of the three emerging generations today.

SECTION ONE

Who and What Are We Talking About?

CHAPTER TWO

Millennials (1980-1996)

Before we dive into how to help youth and young adults on their faith journey, let us take some time to build a critical foundation on what we mean when we say "younger generations." We know that our churches are aging and shrinking, but where are the young adults going, and why do they not want to come to church anymore? Before we look at the *wheres* and *whys* of this issue, let us begin by learning more about *who* we are talking about. We will start with those young adults born between 1980-1994, known as Millennials (Rachel and Kris are both Millennials).

According to sociologists like Mark McCrindle, Millennials were born between 1980 and 1994. Pew Research puts the cutoff age a little later, in 1996. Several defining changes and events have shaped and impacted the identity of this generation.

Reality TV

Millennials were the first generation to experience "reality TV" in 1992 with the launch of MTV's "The Real World," which documented the lives of six strangers picked to live in a loft together. By 2003, the Emmys had added a "reality TV" category to award this increasingly popular form of entertainment. Fast forward to March 16, 2024, the streaming platform Netflix boasted 164 reality TV shows that their subscribers could stream anytime. While almost half of reality TV shows include some form of competition that does not lend itself to "watch parties," there is a growing movement of in-person and online social groups or gatherings that meet consistently to watch, for instance, "The Bachelor," "Real Housewives," or "Married at First Sight" series. Reality TV is literally bringing younger generations together on a regular basis.

Social Media

While scholars and sociologists continue to debate whether reality TV actually depicts *real* life, it is connected to another pivotal shift in the early 2000s: the birth of social media. Younger generations might be "digital natives" born in a Wi-Fi, iPhone, and social media-infused world, but Millennials are known as the "bridge generation." They (Millennials) are the last generation born before the Digital Age, so computer usage in their classrooms was probably limited to playing the game of *The Oregon Trail*. However, by the time they entered adulthood, cell phones and Google were the norm. While Millennials may have had access to cell phones, the most popular social media platform during adolescence was MySpace. By the time they entered college or the workforce, Facebook and Twitter were on the scene.

Same-Sex Marriage

Another defining societal change was the 2004 legalization of same-sex marriage in Massachusetts. The Supreme Court later preserved this right at the national level in 2015. This ruling marked a shift in the protection and acknowledgment of the rights of the LGBTQIA+ community. According to Pew Research, Millennials were the first generation to offer widespread support to same-sex marriage, with 71 percent in favor of it, compared to 56 percent of Generation Xers, 46 percent of Baby Boomers, and 38 percent of the Silent Generation.[12] Within five years, the Episcopal Church in America splintered over its decision to ordain openly queer clergy, followed by splits in the Evangelical Lutheran Church in America in 2009 and the Presbyterian Church's decision in 2012.

At its global gathering in the spring of 2024, the United Methodist Church (UMC) voted to remove all homophobic language from *The Book of Discipline*, its legal and spiritual guidebook for ministry in the church. With sweeping legislation, the United Methodist Church became a fully inclusive and affirming Protestant denomination, following other mainline denominations in the United States.

Election of President Barack Obama

The fourth defining event occurred in the early 2000s. In 2008, 66 percent of voters under thirty voted for then-Senator Obama and celebrated the first Black United States President.[13] Not only was it a landmark shift in our nation's history, but it reflected the increasing diversity of this generation and their

---

[12] https://www.jstor.org/stable/26556308#:~:text=For percent20example percent2C percent2071 percent20per percent2D percent20cent,Pew percent20Research percent20Center percent2C percent202016.

[13] https://www.pewresearch.org/politics/2012/11/26/young-voters-supported-obama-less-but-may-have-mattered-more/#:~:text=In percent20winning percent20reelection percent2C percent20Barackpercent20Obama,the percent20votes percent20of percent20young percent20people.

desire for hope amid difficult times. Millennials were also a key voting group in ensuring President Obama was elected for a second term. He experienced extremely high support from this generation throughout his presidency, with up to 77 percent approving of his work in office, from establishing affordable health care to creating space for "Dreamers" to become citizens of the United States.[14]

The Great Recession and Occupy Movement

The period between December 2007 and June 2009 became known as the Great Recession. Millennials were hit with economic hardship just as many were entering the workforce. The effects of the recession continue as 74 percent of Millennials feel they face financial hardships that other generations did not experience at their age.[15] The economic struggles of the Millennial generation led them to marry and have children later than previous generations.

In September 2023, *CBS News* reported that roughly 45 percent of eighteen- to twenty-nine-year-olds report living at home with their parents.[16] This data includes both Millennials and older members of Gen Z, but it is the highest rate in seventy years, with an additional 60 percent of eighteen- to twenty-nine-year-olds reporting that they lived with their parents at some point in the past two years. Some leading reasons these young adults remain at home

---

[14] https://www.latimes.com/opinion/op-ed/la-oe-winograd-hais-obama-the-millennial-president-20170116-story.html.

[15] https://www.usatoday.com/story/money/2023/09/26/gen-z-millennials-face-unique-financial-challenges/70910672007/.

[16] https://www.cbsnews.com/news/gen-z-millennials-living-at-home-harris-poll/.

are because they need to save money or cannot afford to live independently.

The Great Recession, in many ways, contributed to another event that shaped the identity of Millennials: the Occupy Movement. Young adults no longer trusted the private sector to look out for the national good, so in November 2011, thousands of young adults took to the streets to protest for change. The first protest was held in Manhattan, but hundreds more protests spread nationwide in the following days and weeks. While economists debate whether or not the goals of the Occupy Movement were accomplished, it was the first experience of a large-scale, organic protest movement that shifted public thought away from the overwhelming support for corporate America.[17]

Shootings and Terrorism

A series of defining events impacting Millennials include the Oklahoma City bombing in 1994, the Columbine shooting in 1999, and the terrorist attack on September 11, 2001. "Active Shooter" drills in public schools might be commonplace now, but they were unheard of when Millennials were in the classroom. The Columbine shooting, where two students killed twelve students and one teacher at a high school in Littleton, Colorado, impacted Millennials and their parents. Parents became "helicopter parents" who hovered and sought to protect their children from a world that felt increasingly dangerous. The Oklahoma City bombing that took the lives of 168 people, including nineteen children in the daycare of the Federal Building, also shook the consciousness of

---

[17] https://time.com/6117696/occupy-wall-street-10-years-later/.

Millennials who were introduced to domestic terrorism. While some Generation Z kids were alive on September 11, 2001, most were too young to remember that day, whereas most Millennials can tell you exactly where they were when they heard about the World Trade Center towers falling or when they even saw it live on television.

Because of the increased fear that their children were unsafe, many Millennials were raised by helicopter parents who sought to control their children's lives and the environment around them to ensure safety. Millennial helicopter parents also tended to over-schedule their kids' lives, but Millennials made a shift when they entered parenthood. Many Millennial parents became "drone" parents, who still hover but also allow their children to guide and direct their extra activities and interests.[18]

Jeff Fromm's firm, FutureCast, polled Millennial parents and found that 61 percent believed that "kids need more unstructured playtime," with less than 25 percent thinking their kids are overscheduled. These parents are more likely than previous generations to have a democratic approach to making decisions in the household. While they are more democratic about decisions, they do not wait to see if their kids want a social media presence. Millennials are the first generation to document most of their children's lives online, with research pending on the results of this decision on younger generations who have a digital footprint before taking their first step.[19]

---

[18] https://time.com/help-my-parents-are-millennials-cover-story/.

[19] https://time.com/help-my-parents-are-millennials-cover-story/.

Millennials and the Church

Now that we have explored some key defining changes and events that show the generational shifts Millennials are making in the world, let us look at their relationship to God and spirituality. Gen X and Boomers raised the Millennial generation. While the *Religion News Service* reports that 80 percent of Gen X and 76 percent of Boomers believe in God, that number drops to 66 percent for the Millennial generation.[20] In addition, only 25 percent of Millennials still attend church every week, a drop from 32 percent in 2006. Millennials were some of the leaders of the "exvangelical" and "deconstructing faith" movements, and they continue to explore their relationship with organized religion. We will go further into the concerns Millennials and other young generations have with the church, but for now, let us learn more about Gen Z.

---

[20] https://religionnews.com/2021/08/30/ok-millennial-dont-blame-the-boomers-for-decline-of-religion-in-america/.

CHAPTER THREE

Generation Z (1997-2012)

Key Characteristics

Generation Z was born between 1997 and 2012. The Apple iPhone was launched in 2007 when the oldest members of this generation were ten years old, so this is the first fully digital generation. They have not experienced a world without smartphones and easy 24/7 access to the Internet.

Gen Zers are also the most racially diverse generation to date, with almost 50 percent identifying as BIPOC (Black, Indigenous, and people of color) and 25 percent identifying as Hispanic/Latino. They are more likely to have a foreign-born parent, LGBTQIA+ parent, or identify as LGBTQIA+ themselves.[21] Being raised by Gen X parents who were concerned about safety, they are less likely to have a driver's license at sixteen, drink alcohol, or have teenage sex.[22] While members of this generation have not lived through as many historical events as Millennials, they have been shaped by the world around them.

---

[21] https://www.britannica.com/topic/Generation-Z.

[22] https://www.businessinsider.com/generation-z-sex-alcohol-driving-study-2017-9#:~:text=A percent2040 percent2Dyear percent20study percent20of,and percent20driving percent20at percent20record percent20rates&text=Today's percent20teenagers percent20don't percent20seem,their percent20peers percent20out percent20on percent20dates.

Impact of Coronavirus

Generation Z has been most greatly impacted by the coronavirus pandemic. When the world shut down for a few years, these children missed high school proms, college graduation ceremonies, and the awkward middle school years that were a rite of passage for older generations. Time will tell how missing out on the rituals of adolescence and early adulthood will continue to impact Gen Z, but it is important to note that this generation has a lot of grief and deep awareness regarding the value of life and friendships. Early research suggests that Gen Z struggled with resilience and mental health issues during the COVID crisis.[23]

Digital Relationships

The COVID-19 pandemic accelerated a shift that began in Gen Z years before the global pandemic: how and where relationships are built. With Generation Z being the first fully digital generation, they use their online prowess to initiate and deepen digital friendships.

Young adults in this generation have spent countless hours playing video games with friends online. They are eager to use Snapchat, Whisper, Discord, BeReal, TikTok, and Instagram to connect with those around them. And unlike Millennials, Gen Z realizes the danger of reality TV and oversharing online, which has led them to a deeper awareness of important boundaries and private digital platforms. For example, Gen Z would rather connect with friends on BeReal, an app that forces them to be more authentic and honest,

---

[23] https://www.ncbi.nlm.nih.gov/pmc/articles/PMC9362676/.

rather than post staged pictures on Facebook for the benefit of their grandparents. They prefer Snapchat because posts are temporary, and the filters allow them to play around with their image and how they are perceived in digital spaces.

Most teenagers we know have multiple TikTok or Instagram accounts; one might be their main account, and the other is personal spam, which is reserved for their most trusted friends, where authenticity feels safer and easier to accomplish. What is the difference? Main accounts are meant for anyone in their social circle, and they post pictures where they feel confident about how they look or the image they are presenting. In contrast, the spam account is an "overflow" space for duplicate photos that aren't as pretty or photos of friends that aren't as aesthetic so you don't want them to be as accessible to a larger social circle. They are also more digitally savvy and realize that multiple TikTok accounts allow them to shape the algorithms, so one account might be their calming account with ASMR (Autonomous Sensory Meridian Response) or relaxing, motivational statements. At the same time, another account may have more entertaining TikToks for them to follow.

I (Rachel) had a fascinating conversation with my 15-year-old son after I saw him interacting with friends on a group FaceTime call. I asked him why he bothered to do a video chat when his phone camera was off most of the time or facing up towards the ceiling. He said, "I didn't want it on my face so my friends couldn't take embarrassing photos of me, but I wanted the camera close by in case I wanted to show something to my friends so they could see it too." I had never consciously thought about friends taking pictures of me against my will and using them against me later. I was heartbroken to hear of

33

this added reality in my kids' lives and also proud that they can navigate this new reality in such a clever way. My son has found a way to maintain closeness with friends while also protecting his image.

Gen Z and Gen Alpha are increasingly "brand" conscious and acutely aware of how the world perceives them. Most Gen Z kids know the right angle for selfies and can spot a filtered picture from a mile away.

Distrust of People and Political Institutions

Another noteworthy shift for this generation relates to where young adults turn for trust and truth. Most adolescents today do not have a common place to turn when they want to know what is really going on in the world. If one is lucky enough to have close friends they feel they can turn to for guidance, they look there. However, with the rise of social media, which is piled with teenage angst and drama, many teenagers may not be so trusting of their peers. This is a microcosm of a larger issue with political institutions.

Donald Trump's presidency and subsequent domination of the Republican Party spans most of the years of this generation's political awareness. When our newest voting generation looks at the political landscape, they see a reality TV star and "nepo"[24] businessman who was elected primarily by Christian nationalists and is a twice-impeached, convicted felon who continues to dominate the Republican Party. Not only do they see the way Trump has used social media to spread harmful propaganda and lies, but they also see the

---

[24] A "nepo baby" is a child of a famous or successful parent, whose own success is believed to be due to their family connections, according to https://www.collinsdictionary.com/us/dictionary/english/connection.

hypocrisy of the church elevating someone with questionable morals and character.

Politics and Voting

The Democratic Party was hoping for a huge turnout of Gen Z voters to help them with a "blue wave" in 2024. That dream did not materialize, although Kamala Harris did receive the majority of Gen Z votes and 62% of the vote from women under 30 years old.[25]

Why didn't we see more impact from Gen Z? A *Washington Post* article notes that Gen Z is one of the generations least likely to vote in upcoming elections because they do not think their vote matters.[26] And the far right is focusing a lot of time and energy on recruiting Gen Z to their beliefs in radicalized ways to ensure a groundswell of support for Republican candidates on election day.[27] And while white, young males voted in higher rates for Trump than pollsters expected (Trump won 56% of votes from white men without college degrees under 30 years old while Harris only received 40% of their vote),[28] it could be because they feel the effects of rising gas prices and grocery costs, or it could be the ongoing systemic sexism and racism that made Vice President Kamala Harris seem like a more threatening choice than the former president. Another election surprise was the increase in the

---

[25] https://www.usnews.com/news/national-news/articles/2024-11-06/how-5-key-demographic-groups-helped-trump-win-the-2024-election.

[26] https://www.wsj.com/story/how-gen-z-became-americas-most-disillusioned-voters-d842ae7a.

[27] https://www.thenation.com/article/society/colleges-gen-z-right/.

[28] https://www.nbcnews.com/politics/yes-trump-improved-young-men-drew-young-women-rcna179019.

Hispanic/Latino vote for Trump, although he did not get the majority of their votes.

When all is said and done, the majority of white women (53%) and white men (59%) in our nation voted for a candidate who has routinely made racist, sexist and homophobic remarks and we will have to reckon with that impact on our nation and the message that sends to our diverse, younger generations. When they look at the US, they see a government more obsessed with regulating women's bodies than saving their lives in a classroom by regulating gun control. For them, gun violence in the United States is a public health crisis.

In 2019, gun injury became the leading cause of death among children from birth to nineteen years. Moreover, the United States has had fifty-seven times as many school shootings as all other major industrialized nations combined, and as Gen Z youth go to school for lock-down drills, they see political forces putting America's love of guns above their safety.[29] They see a Supreme Court full of people they did not vote for and cannot elect making decisions about their bodies, their world (climate control and fossil fuel decisions), and the role of religion in their lives. This realization weakens their faith in a system that cares about the future.

Gen Z sees tax breaks for wealthy people and companies who make money off of harming the environment, all while climate change becomes a real and present danger that they will have to fix someday. Gen Z does not know what news sources are reliable, and they don't trust the government to look out for their best interests. But this generation wants

---

[29] https://publications.aap.org/pediatrics/article/153/4/e2023064311/196816/School-Shootings-in-the-United-States-1997-2022?autologincheck=redirected.

to be heard, so they will use their influence whenever and however they can to mobilize their message for the masses. For example, Kamala Harris' 2024 presidential campaign understood the power of social media and reaching out to younger generations. Harris' "brat summer" trend (inspired by singer Charli XCX's latest album title) fueled the launch of her campaign, and her social media strategy made her seem relatable and relevant to younger generations.[30]

Gen Z and the Church

With all that in mind, Gen Z has a complex relationship with the church. Barna reports that 64 percent of Gen Z has left the church. Stating it clearly, 64 percent of young adults ages twelve to twenty-seven have left the church with little or no intention of returning. A solid majority have left. We always assumed kids would stop attending church during their wild and crazy college years but also assumed they would find their way back after getting married and having children.

As we mentioned in the opening chapter, Barna reports that almost 75 percent of eighteen- to twenty-nine-year-olds who leave the church decide to leave before they turn eighteen. This data means that Gen Z is deciding while they are still living at home, often while still attending a church, that this will not be part of their long-term life trajectory. In addition to leaving the church at a younger age than previous

---

[30] https://www.newsweek.com/genius-behind-kamala-harris-social-media-stragey-1937955. "Brat" is a song released by music star Charlie XCX on June 7th that encourages women to be authentic and confident in themselves. People quickly began using her song with clips and quotes of Kamala Harris to show she is "brat" and when Charlie XCX supported these posts on X (Twitter) to her 3.2 million followers, the Harris campaign used her support to continue the trend. https://www.nbcnews.com/tech/Internet/kamala-harris-brat-meaning-mean-slang-charli-xcx-what-does-hq-rcna163026.

generations, they are also waiting longer to get married and have kids—kids they do not intend to bring to church.

A final glaring issue regarding Gen Z's relationship to the church is that they are part of the most diverse generation in existence, and when they walk in the doors of many churches, they find primarily homogeneous congregations. In the United Methodist Church, for example, 96 percent of congregants are white.[31] How can we grow churches that are more ethnically and culturally diverse? The first step is to name the inherent racism and discrimination in our church history and present reality. Eboni Marshall Turman, a leading black theologian at Yale University, once said, "White Christianity in America was born in heresy."[32] Younger generations want us to name the authentic, true reality that Christianity, as it exists in the United States, is steeped in colonization, racism, and discrimination. Until we do the work of learning about our history and learning from our history, we will not be able to make the shifts necessary to become an intercultural, relevant, healthy expression of church.

---

[31] https://www.christiancentury.org/features/missed-opportunities-umc-general-conference#:~:text=Too percent20scary percent20to percent20mention percent20were,them percent20are percent20over percent20age percent2050.

[32] https://sojo.net/biography/david-p-gushee#:~:text= percentE2 percent80 percent9CWHITE percent20CHRISTIANITY percent20IN percent20America percent20was,did percent20not percent20explain percent20her percent20meaning.

CHAPTER FOUR

Gen Alpha (2012-2024)

Gen Alpha is the first generation to be assigned a Greek letter and includes children born between 2012 and 2024. While the oldest members of this generation are just now entering their teenage years, we are already noticing a few distinctions in this youngest generation.

Key Characteristics

If Gen Z was the first generation to be raised entirely on smartphones and the internet, Gen Alpha is the first generation to be raised with a constant social media presence from birth. One of the latest bestsellers addressing the impact of social media on younger generations is *The Anxious Generation: How the Great Rewiring of Childhood is Causing an Epidemic of Mental Illness* by Jonathan Haidt. Haidt includes important information for both Gen Z and Gen Alpha regarding the impact of technology on these younger generations.

The book's central claim is that "two trends— **overprotection** in the real world and **underprotection** in the virtual world—are the major reasons why children born after 1995 became the anxious generation."[33] Haidt found that the

---

[33] Jonathan Haidt, *The Anxious Generation: How the Great Rewiring of Childhood is Causing an Epidemic of Mental Illness,* (Penguin Press: New York 2024).

increase in depression between 2010 and 2015 in both teenage boys and girls was 150 percent, which means that depression became two and half times more prevalent, according to research from the US National Survey on Drug Use and Health.[34]

The rise in mental health issues is not always understood by parents eager to make their children and families into Internet influencers as soon as possible. The role of "momagers" is a growing trend as moms begin to manage their children's social media profiles and "handles" before they take their first breath. Most parents of our youngest generation are Millennials, who are a bridge to digital natives and more aware of social media platforms than previous generations. Ryan Kaji of "Ryan's World" and Anastasia Radzinskaya of "Nastya" on YouTube have 32 million and 97 million subscribers (respectively), bringing in over 20 million dollars in estimated revenue each year for these twelve and ten-year-olds.[35]

We will see an even greater shift in Gen Alpha's relationship to social media as they grow up and utilize social media platforms their parents do not even know exist. Ashley Fell of the McCrindle Institute notes, "This generation has access to technology and platforms that their parents don't even understand. In many cases, children are making their own decisions and even guiding their parents. They have ownership, authority and influence in the realms they operate and influence others of their own age."[36] My (Rachel's)

---

[34] Haidt, *The Anxious Generation.*

[35] https://www.forbes.com/profile/nastya-radzinskaya/.

[36] Mccrindle.com.au/article/topic/generation-alpha/the-inluences-shaping-generation-alpha/.

thirteen-year-old daughter can make a flyer for a local thrift store in minutes using Canva, much to the amazement of the older volunteers who would spend hours trying to add photos to the flyer and make it visually appealing.

With the COVID-19 pandemic putting most of these children on lockdown during their first few years, they missed out on the in-person social skills many children are exposed to in daycare or preschool. Parents of Gen Alpha babies were torn between hearing pediatricians advise against "screen time" for little ones and living in a world shut off from many forms of in-person interaction. As a result, screens served for many years as an essential babysitter while parents attempted to work or rest during the months indoors. These children did not have the same opportunity to take vacations and experience new places or experience the adventures of new playgroups at the park. Like Gen Z, we are seeing an increase in the levels of anxiety, depression, and overall mental health challenges in our youngest children, and this is a problem not likely to go away in the near future.[37]

Whereas Gen Z began to shift from consuming online content to creating it, Generation Alpha fully embraces its creative role in online spaces. They are the first generation to learn in a classroom alongside artificial intelligence (AI), using it to help them create graphics for their Google slides and outlines or summaries for their reports. While sociologists and psychologists are still exploring the ways Gen Alpha will differ from previous generations, it is clear that there will be distinctions. Strengths noted by author Jonathan

---

[37] https://www.businessinsider.com/gen-alpha-explained-technology-views-mental-health-2023-10.

Haidt are that "they aren't in denial, they want to get stronger and healthier and most are open to new ways of interacting. The second strength is that they want to bring about systemic change to create a more just and caring world, and they are adept at organizing to do so (yes, using social media)."[38]

Gen Alpha and Church

When it comes to the church, this is the most unchurched generation, with very few of their parents encouraging religious involvement from an early age. Due to the pandemic, many of these children attended church virtually, if at all, for years. Thus, the church is not an ongoing presence in their life. As church planters and consultants, we have heard for decades that all we need to do to ensure the church's survival is to bring in young families. The painful and honest reality is that post-pandemic young families are not interested in the over-programming of the church or in attending churches that do not offer basic safety in terms of environment and resources for children.

I (Rachel) recently spoke to a ten-year-old boy from Colorado named Eli, whose parents take him to church a few times a month, even though he claims he is an atheist. When asked if he prefers online or in-person worship, Eli said, "I would prefer to go to church in person because you could see more of the stuff than only one spot on the screen." When asked about God, Eli said, "God is a boy and a girl because I do not think they are just one." Eli explained that his favorite part of church is "being an acolyte because it's fun walking down the aisle with the candle because, like, the other candle

---

[38] Haidt, *The Anxious Generation.*

is over in the other section, so you have to walk to it, and the candle is the light of Christ." When I asked Eli if everyone should go to church, he said, "If they don't want to, then they don't have to. If they believe in something else, then they don't have to. Well, I know, like, Buddhism is reincarnation, and, like, other religions also believe in reincarnation or something else, so people should do what they want."

Even at ten years old, Eli knows other world religions and aspects of their belief systems. If younger generations are interested in cultivating their faith, they do so intentionally and informally. I (Rachel) recently spoke to a twelve-year-old girl in the Southwest about her interest in faith, and she said:

> *I have recently started to explore other forms of Christianity. I was raised to be a Methodist, so that was all I ever knew. As I got older, I learned about how many religions there are and how many kinds of Christians there are. So I wanted to experience what it was like to go to another church. I started with an Episcopal church, then Catholic mass, then a non-denominational church, then a Baptist church. I was learning so much, and I wanted to document my research. I made a Google sheet with all of the churches I've been to. I filled out what the routine was for a service, baptism, communion and what requirements there were to each faith. I immediately ruled out several denominations, but a few others caught my eye. I really liked the Episcopal churches in my area. So after some time to reflect and think about all my options, I asked my parents if they would take me to Episcopal churches more often. My parents were a little skeptical at first, but they grew to love my interest in religion. I grew to learn that not everything about your spiritual journey has to be black and white. It's okay to explore new things—because who knows what you might learn.*

There was a movement in the 1970s called the "seeker-friendly" movement where churches tried to reach young adults with contemporary music and drum sets, but this led to a form of consumer Christianity where people came to church to be entertained. Generation Alpha will not be drawn to glitzy weekly worship. They are curious about spirituality and will explore options around them that resonate with their own identified needs about religious formation. Younger generations want authenticity, substance, and ongoing transformation from their faith communities. And yet, the church must come to terms with the fact that Generation Alpha is the least religious generation, and to cultivate a faithful response, we need to acknowledge the overarching themes within young adults today.

SECTION TWO

So What?

CHAPTER FIVE

Values and Commitment
to Social Justice Matter

Now that we have a good sense of the three emerging generations, it is important to continue unpacking how these generations have a conflicted relationship with the church. We recognize there are some pivotal concerns at play. Young adults today frequently express both a disconnect and frustration over the church's stance on important, critical social issues. For too long, pastors and churches alike have struggled to articulate a beautiful, hope-filled theological foundation that speaks to the values of the emerging generations. To further understand the growing gap between the church and the young adults of today and tomorrow, we must identify the key values of these emerging generations.

Gun Violence

The issue surrounding gun violence and proposed gun control measures is deeply personal for many Americans, especially Millennials and Gen Z. Gen Z, in particular, has grown up practicing active shooter drills, seeing frequent news of school shootings, and feeling the constant threat of gun violence and mass shootings. For these generations, this is not a political issue; it is a matter of safety and justice.

We lament the state of violence in our world today, and we seek greater safety and care. A poll in 2018 from the Pew Research Center found that over 70 percent of Millennials and 64 percent of Gen Z support and desire stricter gun control laws.[39] The church needs to address this significant concern to remain relevant and engaged with younger generations.

Yet, the church often stays silent or aligns (sometimes celebrating) with viewpoints that resist stricter gun laws. There is often no willingness to even engage in fruitful dialogue about how to move forward in an era marred by mass shootings. The topic is too taboo for constructive conversation, especially within the context of the church. For many young people, this silence feels like a betrayal and a complete lack of empathy for the current realities of growing up in the United States today. It is much more likely for someone to die from a mass shooting than from a car accident or plane crash.[40]

Many want the church to understand its prophetic voice in the world. The church is to be a voice for justice and life, advocating for practices and policies to protect vulnerable communities and promote peace. There is a deep desire for the local church to truly embody the profound words of Jesus, "Blessed are the peacemakers, for they will be called children of God" (Matthew 5:9).

---

[39] Pew Research Center, "Gun Control Support Among Generations," 2018. https://www.pewresearch.org/politics/2018/10/18/gun-policy-remains-divisive-but-several-proposals-still-draw-bipartisan-support/.

[40] https://news.northeastern.edu/2022/06/03/children-gun-violence/?utm_source=News percent40Northeastern&utm_campaign=4f704cba73-EMAIL_CAMPAIGN_2022_03_03_02_54_COPY_01&utm_medium=email&utm_term=0_508ab516a3-4f704cba73-278822471.

Climate Change

Climate change is another concern for young adults today that the church fails to adequately consider in its ministry scope. Generations growing up and emerging into adulthood are experiencing firsthand the impacts of climate change. We are seeing more severe storms, rising sea levels, and loss of biodiversity. Due to these significant losses, Millennials and Gen Z are passionate about sustainability and protecting our earth for future generations. According to a recent study by The Harris Poll on behalf of the American Psychological Association, 58 percent of Gen Z and 51 percent of Millennials feel concerned and stressed by climate change.[41] Within this reality, we recognize that the church must deeply consider environmental issues a faithful part of their Christian discipleship.

The reality is that many churches deny the severity of climate change or do not believe climate change is a legitimate concern. In some cases, the churches admit honestly that they are simply apathetic. For emerging generations today, these stances can come across as irresponsible. When these young people consider their own faith orientation, religious convictions, and ideological understandings, they are looking for the church to lead the charge in caring for creation. They understand the biblical mandate to steward the earth well. These younger generations are deeply compelled by Genesis 2:15, where God invites and commands humanity to work and care for creation. They value and appreciate these beautiful

---

[41] The Harris Poll, "Gen Z and Millennials Stress About Climate Change," American Psychological Association, 2019. https://www.apa.org/news/press/releases/stress/2019/stress-america-2019.pdf.

words from our Holy Scriptures, and yet, they see a church landscape that shows little to no concern.

When my (Rachel) new church start moved into a permanent building in 2016, one of the first shifts we made was to bring in coffee cups and spoons from home instead of using disposable cups and plastic stirrers. Our church was in Virginia Beach, and we were aware of the harmful effects of plastic straws on wildlife.[42] The congregation expected the church to take a stance and change its behavior to support and care for creation.

LGBTQIA+ Affirmation

When it comes to LGBTQIA+ acceptance, younger generations are far more inclusive and affirming than previous generations. They have friends, family members, and sometimes themselves who identify as LGBTQIA+ and understand their identity as something good and part of God's unique design for their lives. A Public Religion Research Institute (PRRI) study found that 79 percent of Americans aged eighteen to twenty-nine support same-sex marriage, reflecting a significant shift towards inclusivity among younger generations.[43]

With our emerging generations, almost three in ten (28.5 percent) women identify as LGBTQIA+.[44] For comparison, 12.4 percent of Millennial women and 4.7 percent of Generation X women identify as non-heterosexual. Over one in ten (10.6 percent) Gen Z men identify as LGBTQIA+, roughly double

---

[42] https://www.worldwildlife.org/magazine/issues/summer-2018/articles/a-small-straw-s-big-environmental-impact.

[43] Public Religion Research Institute (PRRI), "Support for Same-Sex Marriage by Age," 2020. https://www.prri.org/wp-content/uploads/2024/03/PRRI-Mar-2024-LGBTQ.pdf.

[44] https://www.axios.com/2024/03/13/lgbtq-identity-us-adults-gallup-survey.

the percentage among Millennial men (5.4 percent). Simply stated, the younger the generations get, the more who identify as LGBTQIA+. This picture of inclusion embraces the beautiful diversity of gender identity as well.

However, many churches still hold exclusionary and harmful views on sexuality and gender, which further drives a wedge between the church and these emerging generations. There is a deep desire for communities (faith and not) to be a place where all people can be embraced as their authentic selves without fear, judgment, or potential rejection. The deep fear exists that the church is not a safe, welcoming place for an LGBTQIA+ person, and, in fact, it can be one of the most harmful places.

So, if the church is one of the most harmful places to be, younger generations will not be interested in church because they are protecting themselves and their peers from any potential harm and exclusion. Homophobic and transphobic churches have marshaled against trans kids in school—banned book lists, etc.—at alarming rates. And when some Christians say, "Hate the sin, Love the sinner," and think it is a way of creating a safe, welcoming space for the queer community, it falls short of the goal. Telling a member of the LGBTQIA+ community that they are welcome in your church while failing to support or affirm their ability to be a church leader or to be in a loving relationship or to marry in the church is not welcoming at all.

Social Justice Movement Growing after George Floyd

After the tragic death of George Floyd in the summer of 2020, the Black Lives Matter (BLM) movement saw a significant resurgence and brought the concerns of racial justice to the forefront in the United States again. For Millennials and Gen Z, these events were not simply something they saw on their social media feeds; they were catalysts for a deeper awareness of systemic injustice and the deep humanity that exists within these tragic situations. Millennials and Gen Z are passionate about social justice and concerned about systemic racism and oppression. So, in turn, they want and expect institutions, including the church, to take a stand and be a voice and active presence in the work toward racial freedom and justice—especially as we recognize how the BIPOC communities have been naming this for decades, especially communities that have had police brutality in them already.

The church's responses to these events have been myriad. Some churches are now vocal advocates for Black Lives Matter, using their platforms to call for justice and reform. Others have remained silent or even critical of the movement, which many younger individuals perceive as a lack of empathy or understanding. This discrepancy has furthered the divide, leaving many young people feeling that the church is out of touch with the realities of racial injustice, systemic oppression, and the growing diversity of persons in the world today.

Scripture calls us to act justly and to love mercy. Micah 6:8 states, "He has shown you, O mortal, what is good. And what does the Lord require of you? To act justly and to love mercy and to walk humbly with your God." Proverbs 31:9 also instructs us to "Speak up and judge fairly; defend the rights of the poor and needy." These biblical imperatives align closely with the values of social justice that young people are championing. Hence, the disconnect often confuses young people when social justice and BLM are criticized within the church. Contradictions are emerging.

The United Methodist Church (UMC) has articulated strong positions on social justice issues through its *Social Principles*. The United Methodist Church's *Social Principles* state: "We recognize racism as sin and affirm the ultimate and temporal worth of all persons. We rejoice in the gifts that ethnic histories and cultures bring to our total life. We commit as the Church to move beyond symbolic expressions and representative models that do not challenge unjust systems of power and access."[45] This Protestant denomination (home for both Rachel and Kris) has clearly articulated a beautiful stance against racism and a commitment to justice and works faithfully to engage in this holy work even in the presence of continued racism. The tension resides between merely acknowledging this profound stance and actively working to fight for justice for our siblings.

According to a 2020 survey by the Barna Group, 74 percent of Millennials and Gen Z believe that the church should address social justice issues.[46] They want the church to be an ally in the fight for equality and justice, to speak truth to power, and to be a source of hope and healing. And yet, many pastors and churches alike are not equipped to faithfully engage in this work, so they simply remain silent.

By embracing these values and clearly committing to social justice, the church can bridge the gap with younger generations. It's about more than statements; it is about taking action, being present in the struggle, and showing that the church is a force for good in the world.

---

[45] *The Book of Discipline*, *"Social Principles"* (The United Methodist Publishing House, 2020) ¶162.A.

[46] Barna Group, "Millennials and Gen Z on Social Justice Issues," 2020. https://www.barna.com/research/black-gen-z-justice/.

Silence on Social Activism

One overarching concern and growing tension is
the church's general silence on social activism. Younger
generations are not passive observers; they are active
protagonists in the desire for change in the world. There is
energy within these emerging generations to seek a world
that is free, just, and beautiful for all humans. And so they
march, boycott, and use social media to organize movements
at lightning speeds. A defining characteristic of Gen Z and
Gen Alpha social-justice makers is how easily and fluidly they
organize while using technology.

This sentiment resonates with Christian theology (a
yearning for the Kindom[47] of God), and they want to see
the church doing the same. They are willing to embrace
ideological perspectives that allow their friends, classmates,
and families to live in a world that is safe, free, and beautiful.
There is a deep longing for more churches and pastors to take
stands, advocate for justice, and reflect an alternative voice of
hope in a conflicted, pained world.

Often, when there is a hesitancy for pastors and churches
to engage thoughtfully and theologically on important social
concerns, it underscores the perception that the church
is irrelevant and does not facilitate a welcoming space for
matters that concern younger generations. There is a desire
for the church to be a community where young people see
their values articulated and acted on. They are seeking an

---

[47] This is not a misspelling of "kingdom." "Kindom" is used intentionally to remove the
patriarchal or colonizing language of "King" to reflect God's beloved community
where all of us are "kin" together.

active and engaged faith, one in which they are willing to get a bit messier for the sake of the Kindom of God.

Bridging the Gap

So, what does all this mean for the church? For the sake of emerging generations and the gospel of Jesus Christ, this means churches and their leaders must examine themselves and explore how to thoughtfully be an active leader and voice in the present world. We must be brave enough not simply to offer "thoughts and prayers" but also be willing to do the necessary prayer and theological reflection to help give voice and perspective on the controversial issues of today—to be a people and leaders who are willing to name and correct injustice and capture the energy of our young adults to be a force for good in the world together.

Churches have the beautiful capacity to create spaces where the young adults of today and tomorrow can feel heard, valued, and understood. By doing this, the church can bridge the gap and build a future where younger generations see the church not as an outdated institution but as a vibrant, relevant community deeply committed to the well-being of all its members and the world. As James Cone, a prominent Black theologian, states, "Theology must be a theology of liberation, a theology that speaks to the poor and the oppressed,"[48] meaning all Christian theology must be a voice for freedom and liberation in the world. This sense of liberation is expressed and seen through Jesus' life, death, and resurrection, which burst forth a new world where the struggles for justice and equality are realized. And once we

---

[48]   James H. Cone, *A Black Theology of Liberation* (J.B. Lippincott Company, 1970).

start listening to the voices on the margins, persons who are oppressed and marginalized, persons with their "backs up against the wall," as Howard Thurman once remarked, we will see the profound connection between the gospel and the values of the emerging generations.

Through listening to these stories and capturing young adults' energy, the church can be a force for good, a place of refuge, and a healing agent in the world. But the church and its leaders must be willing to engage deeply (and not simply reiterate partisan talking points) with the social concerns of today so all can experience the Jesus who liberates and sets people free.

CHAPTER SIX

Connecting Faith to
Daily Lives and Issues

I (Rachel) will never forget my first pastoral care visit. It was 2005, and I had just started serving as a pastoral intern in a small rural church in North Carolina. I received a phone call requesting I visit one of the newest church members, a young woman in her early twenties named "Dina." Dina and her husband were raising two young boys in a trailer park outside town with Dina's mother-in-law, who also happened to be a performer at a local bar like Dina.

When I visited Dina, I learned that a recent terminal melanoma diagnosis had led her back to the church. The first thing she said to me after I introduced myself was, "I'm afraid to die, and I want to know what the Bible says that can give me hope right now." As we talked through the scriptures together, I realized that God's Word was literally a lifeline to this scared mother facing death. I was honored to journey with Dina through the final months of her life, and I still have a ceramic angel in my office that her mother-in-law gave me after Dina's funeral. Young adults want their faith to impact their daily lives and the struggles they face.

One of the main reasons that younger generations are not in our pews is that they do not see how an hour on Sunday mornings will impact the other 168 hours in their week. I (Rachel) stopped at the only coffee shop in a small rural town near Tombstone, Arizona, this week and met four young women from Generation Z (we were the only ones there). We discussed whether teenagers attend one of the many churches in their town, and they said that none of them go to church, and they do not plan to go because they do not see the point. One even shared that her dad is a pastor, but she feels like being a Christian and attending church are no longer synonymous. She feels she is more likely to find people who share her beliefs outside the pews on Sunday morning.

Emerging adults today see themselves as a brand, with everyone watching them to see what kind of influence they will have on society. If the church does not transform them or the world around them in some way, they are not interested in it. We cannot minimize the impact of the "influencer" role on our digital natives.

What is the History of the Influencer Phenomenon?

In March 2024, *The New York Times* published an article on the history of "influencers." The term derives from the Latin word *influere,* which means to "flow in," and was used about the stars, which were said to influence or flow into their surroundings and shape the future of humanity. "Influencer" didn't appear in marketing until the 1960s.[49]

With the rise in social media platforms like YouTube and Instagram, the role of a social media influencer was born, and it has become a multi-billion-dollar industry. Recent

---

[49] https://www.nytimes.com/2024/03/09/insider/influence-word-origin.html).

data suggests that 92 percent of consumers would rather have a personal recommendation from someone they know than more traditional forms of advertising. So, if you are a celebrity, professional athlete, or someone on a social media platform who has gained a following, you have sway over the opinions of others.[50]

Examples of Influencers

Unlike previous generations who felt that you needed degrees, experience, or the wisdom of age to influence the world around you, younger generations live a different reality. One notable Gen Z influencer is Malala Yousafzai, born in July 1992. She became a Pakistani female education activist and 2014 Nobel Peace Prize laureate at seventeen (the youngest laureate in history). Her influence began at age eleven when she wrote a blog under a pseudonym detailing what life was like under the Taliban, which then led to a documentary on her experience a year later. As her influence grew, so did the threat to her life, with the Taliban shooting her in the head in an attempted assassination when she was fourteen.

Young adults are not afraid to influence the world around them when they perceive grave societal injustices. After the brutal murder of George Floyd, young adults around the United States and globally began to protest with the Black Lives Matter movement. At the time, I (Rachel) was living with my family outside Nashville, Tennessee. I attended a rally with over ten thousand people at the capital and was surprised

---

[50] https://www.agilitypr.com/pr-news/public-relations/a-brief-history-of-influencer-marketing-and-2-trends-that-define-its-future/#:~:text=In percent20the percent20mid percent2D2000s percent2C percent20platforms,the percent20form percent20we percent20know percent20today.

to learn that the event had been organized by six teenage girls (aged fourteen to sixteen years old) who had met on Twitter a week before the event. Their first in-person encounter was at the rally, where they hoped a thousand people would show up but were excited to see ten times that amount gather with them to protest the discrimination and police brutality against people of color in the United States. Malala's blog and the Twitter platform helped amplify a message for reform and allowed these young women to influence culture in crucial ways.

Not all influencers attain their status through positive world change; sometimes, they just have a lucky break. Consider Charlie D'Amelio, for example. She was born in May 2004 and decided to post a video of her dancing in 2019 on TikTok, where she has become (as of the printing of this book) the second most followed person on TikTok. Since her dancing debut, she has also been in a Hulu reality series, won Season 31 of *Dancing with the Stars*, and joined the cast of an animated film. She now has two books, a podcast, a nail polish collection, a mattress line, a makeup line, and a clothing line, and she launched a venture capital fund with her parents with 25 million dollars. Charlie D'Amelio follows in the footsteps of one of the oldest Millennial influencers, PewDiePie.

Felix Arvid Ulf Kjelberg, aka PewDiePie, was born in October 1989 in Sweden. In 2010, he started a YouTube channel that recorded him playing video games, and it quickly became one of the fastest growing channels in 2012 and 2013. By August 2013, it was the most subscribed YouTube channel and was the most viewed from December 2014 to February 2017. PewDiePie began diversifying his content, including vlogs, comedy shorts, formatted shows, and music videos. In 2019, the most subscribed channel had 111 million subscribers and 29.2

billion views, which has led to a net worth of 45 million dollars as of 2024.[51] Nara Smith is a recent influencer with the rise of popularity in "tradwives," a new term for a traditional wife. She records herself preparing meals for her young, growing Mormon family, and her videos average 25 million views.[52] This wealthy model, who is married to a model, depicts a version of life that seems simple, effortless, and beautiful— even if it is a lifestyle inaccessible or unrealistic to the experience of most stay-at-home parents.[53]

Influencing Faith

Younger generations look at these influencers and realize that anyone with access to technology, a blog, Twitter, YouTube, or TikTok can profoundly shape the world around them. From advocating for social justice issues to developing a brand that allows them to produce more content and make money from views, they see the immediate impact of young voices around them. Similarly, when these younger generations look at the church, an institution that has existed for thousands of years, they do not see the larger impact of a Sunday morning worship service or Wednesday night youth program. What difference does one hour a week make in their life or the lives around them? If we cannot show relevance and impact in what we are doing as a faith community, young generations will find it elsewhere.

---

[51] https://www.yahoo.com/entertainment/pewdiepie-net-worth-2024-much-193800000.html.

[52] https://www.gq.com/story/lucky-blue-nara-aziza-smith-gq-hype.

[53] https://www.npr.org/2024/01/28/1227453741/trad-wives-are-trending-what-does-that-say-about-feminism-today.

Living into a relevant faith is not antithetical to our religious history and scriptural foundations. Jesus spoke in parables, highlighting key principles of faith by using everyday things and situations. Christ's teachings showed how something small or seemingly unimportant, like one lost coin, sheep, or a grain of mustard seed, could have deep salvific meaning. Jesus was an influencer. This one divine man was able to influence a core group of leaders who started a movement that has gone global and continues to proclaim a message of hope, love, and reconciliation. We need churches willing to embrace ethical evangelism and influence the world around them in positive, life-giving ways.

Howard Thurman, the first dean of Rankin Chapel at Howard University and later the first Black dean at Boston University's Marsh Chapel and a mentor to Martin Luther King, Jr., once said, "Don't ask yourself what the world needs. Ask yourself what makes you come alive, and go do that, because what the world needs is people who have come alive." The key to reaching younger generations is not to try to be something you are *not*; it's about letting your faith come alive and influencing the world around you because the joy and passion of your faith cannot be contained.

I think we underestimate how frequently young adults are trying to connect their faith with daily struggles. Bennett, a fifteen-year-old in Phoenix, recently shared:

> *Middle/high school years are hard. I cannot be nice and love everyone, which as a Christian makes me feel guilty, but as a human I feel normal. Weekly, I am faced with the question: how far does God's forgiveness reach? This leads me to wonder how and how much I must change. These questions are hard to answer, and most people my*

age have these questions but not the trust to seek advice from religious leaders. I know this because I have Jewish, Catholic, and Atheist friends. All in all, none of us have a clear and major stance on religion and who is "right." I just know that I want to know God and to have an enjoyable afterlife, and I wonder how there's a separation of heaven and hell if no one is inherently evil. Since this is true, how bad could hell be? I don't plan on seeing this myself, but it is questions like these that keep me up at night after I pray for good hair and a slim waist.

Emerging generations have serious questions about faith, and they want to be a part of a spiritual family that can help them find answers for how to change, how to live, how to love, and how to find peace with themselves and others.

So What Can We Do about the Influencer Phenomenon in the Church?

1. **Create a permission-giving environment** so youth and young adults can begin influencing the church now. Invite younger generations to read scripture, share their faith story, record a podcast with their youth director, or lead a mission project if they are passionate about getting involved. Provide healthy accountability and scaffolding so they can lead without legal or ethical liabilities (for example, minors should not be filling out paperwork to sponsor a 5k run or protest, but they can be the "emcee" of the event, or minors should not put their personal social media handle on posts to church social media platforms because they could be trolled or predators could find their individual social media accounts and Direct Message the minor), but give them a voice in the church now.

2. **Examine your traditional forms of worship** and explore ways you can connect Sunday morning worship to every other day of the week. Perhaps you text a daily reminder with ways to live out forgiveness or compassion in that moment or create a church TikTok or Instagram account that's well-branded and highlights the lives being changed through the church.

3. **Review your church calendar** to discern if the only real option for gathering is on Sundays. How can you nurture the faith journey of young adults daily and help them connect to rituals or practices that influence them in positive ways?

4. **Ensure that you have a presence on the platforms** that your emerging generations are using so you can connect to them in their digital spaces (YouTube, Instagram, TikTok, Discord, or other new emerging apps). Facebook is only utilized by your oldest Millennials, so if that is all you are using, you are not connecting with the youngest generations.

5. **Be authentic.** Younger generations can spot insincerity from a mile away, so do not post messages or pictures that are not true to who you are. Do not use stock photos on your website showing a young and diverse congregation if you are predominantly old and white. Post loving prayers or words of encouragement from a grandparent's perspective instead of trying to sell yourself as the most edgy young church in town.

6. **If you are trolled on social media** (i.e., someone intentionally comments on a post to upset others), be loving in your response and always try to reach out via DM (Direct Message) to begin a conversation with anyone questioning your content.

The church can empower younger generations to leverage their desire to impact the world while embracing sacred faith traditions that give a roadmap for inclusion, justice, and peace. As John Legend once sang, "It takes the wisdom of the elders and the young people's energy"[54] to change the world. To create this level of change, there needs to be a high level of trust and integrity in our clergy leadership and church communities.

---

[54] John Legend and Common, *Selma*, "Glory" (Columbia Records, 2014).

CHAPTER SEVEN

Lack of Trust in the Church and Clergy

Trust. For many followers under 40, the church and religious leaders (i.e., clergy) have not been trustworthy. Broken trust has shattered the view of organized religion and its leaders for many young and emerging adults. This lack of trust is not unfounded, and we resonate with the horror of news accusations and founded cases of abuse in the church. There are real stories, experiences, and pain that must be shared. To consider how the church may be in a more effective relationship with emerging adults, we must first acknowledge and give voice to the harm done within the church.

Acknowledging the Harm

We celebrate the fact that the church and clergy have provided profound comfort and community for many people. As the body of Christ and a collection of faithful followers of Jesus, the church has been a beautiful space for people to encounter the divine. However, this same community and its leaders have also caused deep hurt and feelings of betrayal for many others. As much as it makes us uncomfortable and self-reflective, we cannot ignore this reality. At times, the church has failed to be a safe place. We have failed to protect, nurture, and love in the way Christ invited us to.

Inspired by the broader #MeToo Movement in 2017, the church had its season of exposure. The #ChurchToo movement sought to expose the issues of abuse, especially sexual abuse and general misconduct within religious circles. Many courageous survivors shared their stories, exposing dark experiences where abusers caused harm to innocent people. This movement in 2017 and beyond highlighted more than individual acts of harm. It also shed light on systemic issues within the church, how many church structures sought to keep abuse unchecked and often sought to hide the realities of harm from their larger communities. It cannot be understated that the #MeToo Movement is one of the most defining characteristics of the Millennial generation.

Statistics on Trust and Clergy

According to a Gallup poll in 2020, there has been a stark decline of trust in religious leaders and organizations.[55] This study painfully acknowledged that only 36 percent of Americans trust the church or its leaders.[56] This significant drop is felt among young generations. A 2018 Barna study found that only 24 percent of Millennials trust that church leaders act in the best interests of their church members.[57] These numbers are sobering realities for any church or ecclesial leader today. The reality remains: there is skepticism and mistrust in the very communities and towns where clergy and churches are seeking to impact for good.

---

[55] Gallup, "Confidence in Organized Religion," 2020.

[56] Gallup, "Confidence in Organized Religion," 2020.

[57] Barna Group, "The State of Pastors," 2018.

Impact on the Effectiveness and Integrity of the Gospel

What is most important to acknowledge is that these realities—church harm and lack of trust—directly impact the effectiveness, integrity, and growth of our local churches. If there is a general sense that the church and clergy are not to be trusted, the church has a broken ability and compromised position to witness to Jesus' love and justice. The gospel of liberation, love, justice, and peace may be met with views of suspicion.

In his letters found in the New Testament, Paul often wrote about the importance of integrity in leadership and ministry. In 2 Corinthians 6:3, he writes, "We put no stumbling block in anyone's path, so that our ministry will not be discredited." Trust and integrity are absolutely essential for effective ministry in general and especially with young adults today. Without acknowledging the need for greater integrity, the church weakens its witness, and often, its mission is hindered.

While working toward greater trust and integrity cannot be solely centered on improving the church's brand or image in a community, it can restore credibility and build bridges of understanding, healing, and reconciliation. To appeal to and connect with younger and emerging generations, churches and church leaders must ensure that the message of Christ's love and justice is being communicated and experienced with integrity.

Stories of Trauma and Harm

Speaking to any young adult today, we may quickly hear a story of trauma, harm, or irrelevance about the church. We find it important to foster space for these stories to be heard and understood.

Kaitlynn's Story

Kaitlynn's story powerfully exemplifies how trust in the church can be deeply damaged by the actions of its leaders. A twenty-nine-year-old white woman from Virginia, Kaitlynn never fully understood the concept of "church hurt" until she experienced it herself. She had invited her pastor into her home during a difficult time, seeking pastoral care and support. However, four months later, that same pastor turned his knowledge of her living situation against her, refusing to marry her and her boyfriend because they were living together before marriage. He went further, telling her that she was "living in sin" and unfit to lead a small group in the church.

This harsh judgment left Kaitlynn questioning her worth as a Christian. She was devastated, asking herself if she was "not a good enough Christian" or if she was unworthy of being a role model for others. The pastor's refusal to understand the reasons behind her choices, such as the need to escape an unhealthy home environment and the financial and emotional security of living together, only deepened her hurt. The pastor projected a rigid line of criticism without empathy for her difficult situation, which, unfortunately, resulted in her feeling less than worthy in the eyes of the church.

Despite this, Kaitlynn knew she was enough in God's eyes, but the shame and rejection she felt from her pastor led her and her now husband to leave the church, a heartbreaking decision for them. As someone (Rachel) who pastored Kaitlynn during her teenage years and witnessed her deep faith and desire to serve others, it was devastating to hear about this experience in her first church home as a young adult.

70

Leanne's Story

Leanne reflects on her lifelong relationship with the church with a mixture of emotions. Growing up in a Christian home, church was a central part of her family identity. She found comfort in youth group and summer camps, where she found a deep connection to God and a church community. However, her relationship with the church began to fracture when she went to college and could not find a new church home that felt like her childhood church.

Returning to her home church after college, Leanne found it had changed and no longer felt like a second home. Her search for a supportive church environment continued, but she faced judgment and rejection instead. When she sought premarital counseling at her mother's church while pregnant with her second child, the pastor refused to marry her unless her fiancé moved out of their shared apartment. This left Leanne feeling ashamed and unsupported during a vulnerable time, as this was an unrealistic expectation at this moment in her life.

Years later, while attending a local mega-church, Leanne dedicated herself to serving in the children's ministry, particularly focusing on families with special needs children. Despite her dedication, when she went through a divorce and sought support for her daughters, the pastor told her, "We do not do that here." Feeling abandoned again, she prayed for a church that would truly care for and support her family. She eventually found such a community in The Journey Church, where she and her daughters felt welcomed and valued.

The church should be safe and accepting, where love and

support are expressed first. Yet, Leanne experienced judgment and a lack of support; right doctrine was more important than right relationship.

Christian Nationalism and the Church's Integrity

In addition, when the church and religious leaders entangle themselves too closely with extreme and harmful politics, further erosion of trust in the church happens. This practice has been experienced most notably through the lens of Christian nationalism. The church has, at times, rigidly aligned itself with political ideologies that have compromised and threatened its prophetic voice for people, especially our marginalized and oppressed siblings in the world. At times, in its grasp for power and privilege, Christianity's witness has been compromised by the powers of this world.

Dr. Martin Luther King, Jr., in his "Letter from Birmingham Jail," warned against the church becoming "an archdefender of the status quo" instead of fulfilling its role as a "thermostat that transforms the mores of society."[58] The church must maintain its integrity and independence to challenge injustice and advocate for the marginalized effectively.

At its worst, Christian nationalism conflates one's religious and national identities. The focus centers on the notion that to be a good Christian is to support a specific political agenda—basically assuming that to be Christian is to vote for one party or person rather than being a voice that seeks to influence our political sphere. For many, the

---

[58] Martin Luther King, Jr., "Letter from Birmingham Jail," 1963.

church has become a tool used for political ends rather than a transformative force working for the good of all humanity.

Jesus made a clear distinction between the Kindom of God and earthly powers. In John 18:36, he stated, "My kingdom is not of this world." The church's primary allegiance and focus must be to the values of the Kindom of God that seek to unite and empower all people—values of love, justice, and mercy. Throughout the Sermon on the Mount in Matthew's Gospel, we hear about the Kindom of God that is countercultural to the values of the earth. Jesus is not simply giving moral commands for humanity; he is unveiling a whole new way to be human. A lighter, more free way to be human.

In a time when anger, violence, retaliation, and verbal vitriol are the norm—where racism, sexism, homophobia, Islamophobia, anti-Semitism, and transphobia are part of our earthly ethos—Jesus ushers in a new Kindom of Love. In this new Kindom, love shows no hostility and does no harm, love is truthful and kind-hearted and does not retaliate, and love extends to our enemy. This Kindom is not part of one political party. Christian nationalism seeks to give power and voice to only a few powerful people in America, for instance, only persons who are white. In the Kindom of God, love extends to the beautiful diversity of ALL God's creations.

Practical Steps for Rebuilding Trust

We believe in the power of reconciliation and rebuilding trust in relationships. Here are some practical steps for churches and leaders to consider as we work towards rebuilding trust with younger generations.

1. **Transparency and Accountability**: Establish clear policies and procedures for addressing misconduct and abuse. Ensure that these policies are communicated openly and followed rigorously.

2. **Active Listening**: Create open, safe environments where people can share their stories and be heard without judgment. This can include support groups, counseling services, and open forums for dialogue.

3. **Consistent Messaging**: Align the church's teachings with its actions. Address social justice issues, support marginalized communities, and demonstrate a commitment to living out the values of the Kindom of God.

4. **Education and Training**: Provide regular training for church leaders and members on topics such as abuse prevention, LGBTQIA+ inclusion, and racial justice. Equip your faith community with the knowledge and tools to create a safe and inclusive environment.

5. **Restorative Practices**: Implement restorative justice practices that focus on healing and reconciliation. This can include facilitated dialogues, public apologies, and reparative actions to address past harms.

Rebuilding Trust: A Prayer of Lament

One way to rebuild trust is to begin with honesty and humility: acknowledge the pain that has been experienced in religious circles and by clergy and lament the harm done. We invite you to pray the prayer of lament that follows and to sit in the pain and seek restoration. May it be a source of healing for your leadership and your faith community as well. May this prayer of lament also help us express our sorrow, seek forgiveness, and commit to change together.

Prayer of Lament

O God, we come before you with heavy hearts,
Acknowledging the pain and hurt caused by your church.
We lament the stories of abuse, betrayal, and neglect,
The voices that have been silenced, the trust that has been broken.
Forgive us for the times we have failed to act justly,
For the times we have turned a blind eye to suffering,
For the times we have prioritized power over compassion.
We lift up the voices of those who have been harmed,
We hear their cries and commit to walking alongside them in their healing.
Help us to rebuild trust, to be a reflection of your love and justice,
To embody a church that is a sanctuary for all.
In your mercy, heal our brokenness,
And guide us on the path of reconciliation and renewal.
Amen.

Moving Forward with Hope

Acknowledging the reality that the church and clergy have caused harm is not easy. And the journey toward rebuilding trust with our communities is not easy either, but it is essential for the future of the church. We invite you to acknowledge the harm done, listen to the stories of pain in your communities, and work to create steps toward concrete change. We pray for the healing of those harmed and for new practices and leadership to promote healing, justice, inclusion, and hope in the world. Through this, we believe the church will be a more credible witness and foster a better relationship with the younger generations emerging today.

SECTION THREE

Now What?

CHAPTER EIGHT

Creating an Intergenerational Church

The hardest step is realizing that to reach young adults, we need to do more than change the type of coffee we serve or what we post on social media. The following five principles will impact every aspect of your church's life. These principles may elicit anger, confusion, or grief at some of the changes that need to occur, but there can also be great hope, love, and energy when we start living into our call to be an intergenerational church for all God's people. As you read through the next five chapters, take notes and pray over them, discerning how to implement these changes into your own context.

You might say that the "ask" here is too much, but these young adults have left the church slowly, over decades, because of principles and people that have led them away. These young people have left the church because they have not seen comprehensive, transformative, relational discipleship systems that have changed the lives of the Christians in their midst. These young people left the church because the values God seems to value most (love for all, care for creation, and compassion for our neighbors) are not values of God's churches. The changes required from local churches are substantial because we have slowly walked away from the difficult path of regularly sacrificing our comfort and ways of being to reach those who do not yet know God's love.

My (Rachel) two favorite quotes to share with churches discerning whether or not it is worth the risk of changing and adapting are a quote from C.S. Lewis's *Screwtape Letters* and a quote from Archbishop William Temple. *The Screwtape Letters* is a series of letters that a "tempter," or demon named Screwtape, writes to a less experienced demon named Wormwood to help him with a "Patient," or person he is trying to keep from the Kindom. In one letter to Wormwood, we read, "Indeed the safest road to Hell is the gradual one—the gentle slope, soft underfoot, without sudden turnings, without milestones, without signposts."[59] We have to change so much about our churches because we did not realize that slowly, over months, years, and decades, the church shifted from an outward focus to an internal one. We have shifted from being a "city on a hill," shining God's love and grace to others to a campfire for our closest friends where we keep warm and tell stories that draw us closer to each other.

Because it's been a gradual shift over time, it's hard to realize how far we've drifted from the initial call of Christ to leave the ninety-nine and go after the one lost sheep. Is it a sacrifice? Yes! Is it worth it? Yes! Am I saying that all churches are on a slow descent to hell? No, but I am mindful that so many of us have lost our way. That experience isn't unique to this modern church era. Ephesus, located in modern-day Turkey, is still one of the best-preserved ancient cities in the eastern Mediterranean. In Revelation 2, we read these words to the church in Ephesus:

---

[59] C.S. Lewis, The Screwtape Letters (HarperOne, 2015).

*I know your deeds, your hard work and your
perseverance. I know that you cannot tolerate wicked
people, that you have tested those who claim to be
apostles but are not, and have found them false. You
have persevered and have endured hardships for
my name, and have not grown weary. Yet I hold this
against you: You have forsaken the love you had at
first. Consider how far you have fallen! Repent and do
the things you did at first. If you do not repent, I will
come to you and remove your lampstand from its place.*

Revelation 2:2-5 (NIV)

So many of our churches have persevered and endured
hardships but have forgotten their first love. In Matthew 22:36,
we read that the greatest commandment is to love God with
all our heart, mind, body, and soul and to love our neighbor
as ourselves. My friends, our neighbors are not just the people
who sit beside us on Sunday mornings. They are the ones who
don't know that they are welcome in your pews.

Archbishop William Temple once said, "The church is
the only institution that exists primarily for the benefit of
those who are not yet members." My (Rachel) worship leader
in Virginia Beach, Andy Gilstrap, shared that quote with
me in the first few years of starting a new church there. As
we grew from dozens of young adults to hundreds of people,
I was tempted to focus our decisions on what the growing
congregation wanted instead of what the surrounding
community was craving. It is incredibly difficult to look at
people in the pews who have become your church family and
put the needs of those who do not attend church before your
beloved friends. But if the disciples had focused on keeping
each other happy, building up the church in Jerusalem, or
systematizing Sunday morning worship to one particular

81

format, none of us would be here today.

Mark 16:19-20 says, "After the Lord Jesus had spoken to them, he was taken up into heaven and he sat at the right hand of God. Then the disciples went out and preached everywhere, and the Lord worked with them and confirmed his word by the signs that accompanied it." The disciples traveled from Jerusalem to Damascus, to Antioch and Asia Minor, to Greece and Rome, and their goal was to share the story of Jesus and form communities of belonging. Ultimately, what you will read in the coming chapters is similar to their journey. We encourage you to find new ways to share the gospel that resonate with the deepest longing of curious, young minds. We remind you of how belonging is forged, inside and outside the church, and how to form a community founded in love, not judgment.

We invite you to consider recreating spiritual practices that have shaped the church for centuries and work to revive your church in this modern age. Do not see the following chapters as a simple checklist (although there are suggestions for what these changes might look like throughout each chapter). See them as an invitation to reconsider all you are doing and how you are doing it. See it as a means to explore new ways of being and loving your younger neighbors.

CHAPTER NINE

Create Spaces for Questions, Curiosity and Doubt

In the previous chapters, we explored how the church has struggled to connect with younger generations. From differences in values to the church's silence on crucial social issues to a concern that the church has no real impact on their daily life and a lack of trust in the church and clergy, it is ever apparent that traditional methods and approaches are no longer working effectively. So, the quandary leads us to questions: How do we respond to these problems? What effective mind shifts are needed to address the gap between the church and younger generations? What wonderful new things are emerging that are giving space and freedom for young adults in the life of the church today?

The reality is we will not fix any of this overnight. And yet, there are ways to begin reimagining the life of the church to engage effectively and beautifully with younger generations. One powerful way to engage younger followers is by creating safe environments where questions, curiosity, and doubt are not only welcomed but encouraged.

Safety: A Place to "Exhale"

Creating a sense of safety within the church is paramount. Safety means more than just physical well-being; it encompasses emotional, spiritual, and psychological security. It is about creating an environment where individuals can "exhale" and be themselves without fear of judgment or exclusion.

We live in a world with an unruly number of expectations showered upon us: expectations to achieve the American dream, climb career ladders, have "perfect" families, have a perfect relationship with God, and so much more. Many of us are trying to juggle the expectations of our partners, families, employers, and those we place on ourselves. At times, this leads people to a tired, worn-out place. Humans are deeply in need of a safe community.

Psychologist Abraham Maslow was one of the first to identify this need. In his famous hierarchy of needs, Maslow recognized that before people can feel a sense of love and belonging, they must first feel safe.

In our safety, we are allowed to be *all* of ourselves, encompassing the good and the bad, the joy and the sorrows, and even the quirkiest versions of ourselves. Through safety, amid an isolated world, people can finally find belonging, connection, and purpose in their lives. Through this safety and belonging, they can unpack and discover this incredible God who has started good works within them (whether they realize it or not)!

Safety embodies a community value where no one gets left behind. Christianity is always an open invitation. Jesus always invites others into a life-giving way of being, but the choice is ours to make. We can choose to say yes to living in a bigger tent where all are honored, valued, and experience safety by being a part of our faith community. As the Reverend Doctor Jacqui Lewis states, "Everything—my spiritual maturation, my grown-up faith, my preaching, teaching, writing, activism, and advocacy—all would become a quest to leave no one behind … and build a wider tent for myself and others, so we would get to healing and liberation together."[60]

Safety looks like leading a youth program that allows students to be honest about their faith, sexuality, fears, and worries and know that their authentic selves are not too scary or threatening to the leaders and pastors. Safety looks like an adult who has never been in the church being invited to belong before they fully believe. Safety looks like a person naming their addictions and the ways they have harmed their marriage, and they are, in turn, fully embraced and held. Safety leads people to experience the best possible community—the community of imperfect people worshiping a perfect God and pushing each other toward radical honesty.

In his book *Radical Love*, queer theologian Patrick S. Cheng emphasizes the importance of inclusivity in theological spaces. He writes, "Christian theology at its best is radically inclusive and life-giving for all people, including LGBTQ individuals."[61] This inclusivity is essential for creating a safe environment where everyone feels valued.

Safety means providing spaces (one could even say a sanctuary) where people are invited and allowed to bring their full selves—their doubts, questions, fears, hopes, and dreams—to the table. They are invited to show up "as

---

[60] Rev. Dr. Jacqui Lewis, *Fierce Love: A Bold Path to Ferocious Courage and Rule-Breaking Kindness That Can Heal the World* (HarperOne, 2021).

[61] Patrick S. Cheng, *Radical Love: An Introduction to Queer Theology* (Seabury Books, 2011).

themselves" in the fullest, and the church is never content until people are invited to bring their fullest selves. To name this theologically, Jesus interacted with people in a way where people were fully known, seen, and understood. Creating space for safety is truly embodying Jesus' values and ministry.

Safe Spaces vs. Brave Spaces

There is a distinction worth repeating between creating a "safe place" and a "brave place." A safe space allows for vulnerability and authenticity. A brave space challenges people to engage deeply in difficult conversations and confront their uncomfortable truths. Both brave and safe spaces are needed to embody a dynamic, transformative faith community and spiritual journey.

Brave spaces require us to ask hard questions and challenge the status quo. James Baldwin, a pivotal African American thinker, noted, "Not everything that is faced can be changed, but nothing can be changed until it is faced."[62] Creating brave spaces means fostering an environment where difficult questions can be asked and people are given space to journey through life and their spirituality. As vulnerability writer Brené Brown shares, "We cultivate love when we allow our most vulnerable and powerful selves to be deeply seen and known, and when we honor the spiritual connection that grows from that offering with trust, respect, kindness, and affection."[63] Brave spaces within our church communities are essential in inviting someone to express their most authentic selves rooted in trust and respect.

---

[62] James Baldwin, *The Fire Next Time* (Vintage Books, 1963).

[63] Brené Brown, *The Gifts of Imperfection* (Hazelden, 2010).

Safety is foundational to one's psychological well-being, and yet, brave spaces push us to places of growth and transformation. It is like the difference between spending a day in a cozy living room and spending time at the gym. One allows us comfort, safety, and rest, and one invites us to be challenged and stretched. Both are essential to living.

For me (Kris), one favorite aspect of pastoring in Harrisburg is leading from a place of vulnerability and truth-telling. It is not uncommon for me to acknowledge my own questions, doubts, and fears as they relate to our Holy Scriptures and the life of being a Christian. It is not uncommon for us to be reading the words and stories of Jesus, and I insert my own wonderings about this inspiring, wandering preacher named Jesus. I ask questions and share my doubts, but not to mislead or distract us from experiencing the divine in our worship gatherings. Rather, I seek to model that asking good and faithful questions is part of the Christian journey and that it is indeed in the asking of probing, thoughtful questions that we are led to know more about this God of our ancestors and the God who is living and leading us today. In order to ask such questions, there needs to be space for safety and bravery in our faith communities.

What Does It Mean to Create Safety?

To create safety, we must know and understand the very people God has called us to be in relationship with. We must know their fears, hopes, needs, and distinct generational framework. This is why we felt compelled to write this book: We believe in the power of building trust and showing genuine care to an emerging generation that deserves to know about the liberation of Jesus and to be understood by aging pastors and churches.

To embody this type of mutual relationship, established churches and pastors must create safe spaces where young adults can be fully seen and understood. It goes beyond offering a warm welcome; it embodies a community and conversation space for ongoing relationships where young adults feel known, loved, and valued.

Curating Spaces with Intentionality

This kind of safe space sounds great in theory but does not simply happen by accident. It requires great intentionality, careful thought, and curation. In her book *The Art of Gathering*, Priya Parker stresses the importance of intentionality in creating meaningful gatherings. She writes, "Gathering, when done well, helps people find a sense of belonging."[64]

Churches and faith leaders must embrace the words of Parker and recognize our inherent power and privilege in fostering spaces of belonging and community. We are invited to create environments in our religious institutions for curiosity, openness, and wonder.

A theological framework and conviction that embraces doubt and curiosity is vital for younger generations. Too often, churches and their leaders have emphasized certainty, doctrinal purity, and structural survivability and hindered exploration, questioning, and doubts, leaving little room for the real dynamics of life and curiosity. Sometimes, we

---

[64] Priya Parker, *The Art of Gathering: How We Meet and Why It Matters* (Riverhead Books, 2018).

might acknowledge that curiosity and doubt are integral to a vibrant faith journey but leave little room in our lived practice for uncertainties.

In the Gospel of Mark, a father brings his son to Jesus, seeking healing. He cries out, "I do believe; help me overcome my unbelief" (Mark 9:24). In the gospel of Jesus, there is always space for doubt, recognizing that faith and doubt can coexist. We believe that a core strategy in connecting with younger generations is the compassionate stance that faith and doubt can coexist. Fostering communities that embrace a theology of curiosity and doubt allows for a richer, more thoughtful engagement with faith and Christianity that can lead toward greater (and longer) engagement with faith. Queer theologian Marcella Althaus-Reid, in her work *Indecent Theology,* argues that theology should embrace the messiness and complexity of human experience, including doubt and uncertainty. They write, "Theology must be indecent, open to the ambiguities and uncertainties of life."[65] This faith is dynamic and growing.

To make this plain, faith should not be a destination (to worship under a steeple on Sundays); rather, it is a beautiful journey with God—a journey that leads the young and old alike to a place where questions are not simply tolerated but affirmed. Faith is about exploring the grand mysteries of God. One of my (Kris) favorite descriptors of God is that God is illimitable. God is without limits, and we, as God's beloved children who are limited in our scope of knowledge, can create beautiful, humble spaces to experience this God. Without this

---

[65] Marcella Althaus-Reid, *Indecent Theology: Theological Perversions in Sex, Gender and Politics* (Routledge, 2000).

orientation, young adults may struggle to have the necessary space and compassion to explore the grand mysteries of God and wrestle with their doubts and faiths.

Building a Culture of Curiosity and Openness

Culture matters. It shapes who we are and how we interact with the world. Creating a church culture that values curiosity, questions, and doubt requires a deliberate shift in how we operate and communicate. It involves setting clear values and modeling them in every aspect of church life.

One of my (Kris) favorite innovative moments in the life of The Journey Church was our summer of "Brunch Church." Jessyca, who had experienced harm from the church, found healing in a community that welcomed her questions and doubts. At one point, she asked me about a Bible passage we were discussing, and I simply responded, "I don't know." With tears running down her face, she named publicly that this was the first time in her spiritual journey that she was given permission by a religious leader to acknowledge uncertainty and doubt. It was also the first time a religious leader admitted to her their own questions and uncertainty about the Bible and the Christian faith.

A sense of relief was expressed throughout this worship experience because we could approach God with our fullest selves and trust that God would meet us amid our doubts and questions. It was a holy space where answers and certainty were not glorified; questions were celebrated, affirmed, and embraced. Brunch Church, an intentional worship expression on a Sunday morning that combined communal meals with open discussions, created a space where everyone could share their stories and explore their faith without fear of judgment.

Through this brunch experience, Jessyca and I gave each other space and grace to be honest with our doubts and questions and wrestle with the Christian faith! And yet, what it led us to was experiencing Jesus deeper.

Creating a culture of curiosity and openness means being intentional about our actions and our words. It means creating environments where young adults feel safe to explore their faith and where their doubts are seen as a natural part of the journey. It means creating a community where everyone feels valued and their voices are heard.

Here are some practical steps and examples for creating spaces of safety, curiosity, and doubt:

1. **Listening Circles**: Organize small group gatherings where people can share their stories and ask questions without interruption. Pass around a tangible object as a "talking piece" to ensure everyone has a chance to speak and be heard. The Journey Church holds various styles of "mixers" for people (either new people or established members) to engage with each other around faith and the life of our church to break down barriers in our community and learn deeper aspects about each other. For example, we gather at a local restaurant or coffee shop with food, drinks, and name tags and create an intentional space to mingle and engage in organic small group conversation for the sole purpose of building relationships. We invite some of our most hospitable people to attend and facilitate conversation with the newer community members.

2. **Open Forums/Discipleship Moments**: Host quarterly discipleship moments (or open forums) centered on difficult topics that can be discussed thoughtfully. This is a common practice in the life

of The Journey, where we host quarterly gatherings on Sunday evenings centered on a difficult topic. We recognize that some difficult topics are a bit too nuanced to limit the discussion to a Sunday morning. So, we gather for three hours on a Sunday evening to discuss. The first hour centers on a presentation, a theological or biblical framework on the subject. The second hour is centered on a panel discussion with subject experts, and the third hour is small group discussions. This structured time together has created a sacred space to encourage critical thinking, a biblical and theological framework, and empathy in our community.

3. **Inclusive Worship Services**: Design worship services that reflect the diversity of your community. Include different voices and diverse commentaries instead of turning primarily to straight, white, male voices. Share different perspectives in the liturgy and create moments for reflection and dialogue.

4. **Brunch Church**: Try incorporating a meal into your gatherings. Sharing food creates a relaxed, welcoming atmosphere where people can open up and engage in meaningful conversations.

5. **Additional Adaptive Space**: At The Journey, we recently discovered the neurodiversity of our church membership, including our children. So now, for instance, we make headphones available for people who are triggered by loud noises. Identify the specific needs of your congregation that invite even greater participation and inclusion.

Embracing Curiosity

Being a part of and leading a community that embraces curiosity and questions is deeply life-giving. It is holy and sacred to lead a community that celebrates questions instead of trying to have all the answers. Imagine holy communities emerging all around where young adults are given space to name their questions and doubts, communities where young adults are met with compassion, empathy, and mutual sharing.

There is indeed space for persons who have been in the church and engaged with faith longer to share wisdom and perspectives, but this space is centered around mutual sharing on the journey of faith filled with its beautiful complexities. As we strive to build communities where younger generations feel safe, valued, and engaged, the journey itself must be seen as sacred. By fostering a culture of curiosity and openness, a space for deeper reflection and an authentic relationship with God and each other emerges.

We imagine and pray for a church where people feel safe to bring their whole selves and where their questions and doubts are seen as a natural part of the journey. We imagine and pray for a community where everyone feels valued and their voice heard. This kind of church will engage and inspire younger generations. This kind of church will make a difference in the world!

CHAPTER TEN

Foster Belonging

"My God, My God, why have you forsaken me?" The cry of dereliction is one of the most painful and controversial crucifixion passages. Not only was Jesus suffering, humiliated, and slowly suffocating on the cross, but he was doing so with a deep sense of loneliness and abandonment. Did God forsake God's only Son? Does Jesus understand what it feels like to be utterly alone in this world in your darkest moment? We are all hardwired for relationships and crave a sense of belonging to a community, especially when we are suffering. We have all cried out in heartache at times, unsure if anyone really cares. So, why are we so lonely?

The Need to Belong

Robert Putnam received national acclaim for his 2020 book *Bowling Alone*, and he is releasing another book in 2024, *Upswing*, that highlights the ongoing and increasing struggle with loneliness in America. In his initial book, he described two types of social capital: bonding and bridging. "Bonding" social capital brings us closer to people who are similar to us, and "bridging" social capital brings us closer to people who are not. In a recent interview with *The New York Times*, Putnam discussed his new book *Upswing* and describes three reasons why we are seeing a continued increase in loneliness, especially among younger generations.[66] And surprisingly, it is not related to our busy schedules.

In fact, Putnam shared that the busier someone is, the more *likely* they are to connect or join others for increased social capital. The reasons he lists for increasing societal loneliness, especially among younger adults, are political polarization, inequality, and morality (in the sense that we no longer believe we have to look out for the interests of others).

When churches create spaces of belonging to draw in isolated young adults, they can create *bridging* social capital that is so hard to find in our modern era. These bridges can transcend political differences, dismantle inequality in our communities, and remind society that we are intrinsically and ethnically connected to each other. And as a result, we have an obligation to care for one another. How many spaces in America have regular opportunities to connect with people from different generational, socio-economic, cultural, ethnic, political, and sexual backgrounds? If we hope to end the polarization in America and beyond, the church must be at the forefront of bridge-building and creating common ground for the common good.

Belonging in a Digital Age

The church plays a crucial role in fostering a sense of belonging, especially with the rise of social media in these digital generations. Jonathan Haidt notes in his book *The Anxious Generation* that when you are in a community that "you cannot easily escape, they do what our ancestors have done for millions of years: They learn how to manage relationships, and how to manage themselves and their

---

[66] https://www.nytimes.com/2024/07/13/magazine/robert-putnam-interview.html.

emotions in order to keep those precious relationships going."[67]

Because it is so easy for emerging adults to "block" or "delete" friends and upend relationships with a click, it is important that the church offer ways for them to stay in relationship with one another in healthy ways that mold and shape us into better followers of Christ and better members of a larger society. Author Jhumpa Lahiri once said, "The essential dilemma of my life is between my deep desire to belong and my suspicion of belonging." When we offer opportunities for authentic faith to be formed and shaped in community, we give younger generations a healthy way to belong to God and each other, and we can help rebuild the trust that they previously lost in the institution of church or church leaders.

What are Millennials Looking For?

Surprisingly, members of Gen Z and Millennials are hungry for more belonging in their lives. Sacred Design Labs recently researched what Millennials are looking for in community, and they uncovered six main criteria that made their determination. They discovered that Millennials use the following criteria to determine if they will be part of something:

1. Community
2. Personal transformation
3. Social transformation
4. Purpose finding
5. Creativity
6. Accountability.[68]

---

[67] Jonathan Haidt, *The Anxious Generation: How the Great Rewiring of Childhood is Causing an Epidemic of Mental Illness*, (Penguin Press: New York 2024).

[68] https://sacred.design/wp-content/uploads/2019/10/DecemberGathering.pdf.

So then we must ask why Millennials are more likely to join a CrossFit Box (gym) with extreme workouts than attend worship on a Sunday morning. Because there's something about that space that gives them a sense of community (people know their name when they walk in the door), personal transformation (who doesn't want to be more fit?), social transformation (competitive workouts to raise money for nonprofits), purpose finding (goal setting is ingrained into Crossfit's mentality), creativity (new workouts and circuits are incorporated all the time), and accountability (they reach out if you do not show up).

Does this mean that the church has to "sell out" and become something it is not to reach these younger generations? No! Hopefully, every church wants to create the community the Apostle Paul spoke of, with the church being the body of Christ and the family of God.[69] As people of faith, we see personal transformation as part of our spiritual faith formation. When we learn to offer ourselves completely to God's will and plan for our lives, we can experience freedom, love, and peace like we have never known before. All churches should be engaged in social transformation.

We (Kris and Rachel) have a mutual friend, Paul Nixon, who has mentored us in ministry throughout the years. Paul taught us to ask a question of every church that invites us to do consulting work around revitalization. The question is: "If the doors of this church closed tomorrow, would anyone notice?" When churches are not engaged in social transformation beyond their doors, they function more like a country club. This reality is not appealing to younger

---

[69] 1 Corinthians 12:12-14.

generations or anyone longing to see a faith community bring healing and hope to their surrounding community.

The Need for Diversity

If Gen Z and Gen Alpha are the most diverse generations in American history, then it is important to incorporate diversity into our faith communities. In her book *Abuelita Faith,* Kat Armas says, "We need one another because no one person or one group of people can fully bear all that is God's image. Instead, each culture, people, or group offers a glimpse of a different aspect of the full image of God."[70]

If we want to create belonging in an increasingly diverse world, we need to be willing to change some of our predominantly white protestant practices with ones that make us more intercultural and intergenerational. This change could look like a plethora of things—such as incorporating different music styles and language, different orders of worship, different digital platforms, and inviting diverse liturgists and preachers to the pulpit. Children could also be invited to sing, play, and be active in the worship space instead of relegating them to children's church. These are simple but thoughtful ways that some church communities are embracing. And for clergy leaders, we need to expand our theological and reading material to include authors and theologians from diverse backgrounds (i.e., a non-white European perspective). Beautifully rich and thought-provoking works of diverse voices can help broaden our understanding of God and God's Kindom.

---

[70] Kat Armas, *Abuelita Faith: What Women on the Margins Teach Us about Wisdom, Persistence and Strength,* Brazos Press, Grand Rapids 2021.

The Need for Creativity

Churches should be the first Google "hit" when someone wants to find their purpose. It is normative for people in the church to hear stories of those who are lost and struggling and hear stories of people who find their calling and unleash their gifts to achieve great things. But the world has not always heard those stories, or they have not been communicated in compelling ways. If churches could find a way to proclaim the stories of Joseph in Egypt, David and Goliath, Queen Esther and Haman, and Mary and Martha and draw lessons from their lives to use as a modern-day guide for finding purpose, you might find more young adults in our pews.

If you see a church with growing numbers of young adults, they are likely a church with worship experiences and discipleship pathways that are creative, compelling, and connected to their lived 24/7 experience. There was a time when people would endure rote and lifeless Sunday morning services with mediocre preaching, but those times are gone.

We serve a creative creator God, who brought all of existence out of nothingness. A God who created the Grand Canyons, the Mariana Trench, the Amazon Rainforest, and the Sahara Desert. God brought animals as strange as giraffes and butterflies, Komodo dragons, and narwhals to life. We serve a God with imagination! We also follow a God who inspires us to use the arts to respond to our faith. The first song in scripture came from the lips of Moses' sister, Miriam, after they had been rescued from captivity in Egypt through the parting of the Red Sea. She sings, "I will sing unto the Lord for he has triumphed gloriously, the horse and the rider thrown into the sea."[71] If you look at the history of Christianity, we have consistently been great patrons or supporters of the arts. Creativity inspires us to see the divine in new ways, and if worship experiences felt more creative on Sundays, we might retain and disciple more of our younger guests.

While this can be exhausting to do weekly, we invite you to gather a team together that helps you put together creative elements on a monthly or regular basis. There were times that I (Rachel) would preach while someone was painting, potting a plant, or knitting a shawl. Other times, we (Rachel and Kris) invited our congregations to mold something with clay, draw something on a poster on the wall, or walk through visual stations of the cross and reflect in interactive ways. These elements took time to plan and execute, but the congregation was more engaged, and their faith in Jesus was emboldened. These examples were ways to personally experience the creative God we worship and helped us transcend a model of Sunday morning solely centered on a monologue. It was not just the younger adults; infusing creativity into our worship services can also positively impact our more senior members.

One January, my (Rachel) ninety-year-old grandmother traveled from her home in southern Illinois to be with me in worship in Virginia Beach. I was nervous because we were doing an interactive Wesleyan Covenant Service for the New Year, and I was not sure what she would think. After worship, she came up to me with tears in her eyes and said it was the loveliest service she had ever attended.

---

[71] Exodus 15:21.

The final thing Millennials are looking for when it comes to belonging is accountability. We will go into depth more on this particular need in a later chapter about reclaiming spiritual disciplines, but it is important to note now that younger generations are looking for deeper friendships and relationships that lead to mutual accountability and respect. When we foster churches where belonging happens, all these elements can be experienced by this emerging generation in ways that compel them to remain followers of Jesus and members of a local church.

What are Gen Z and Gen Alpha Looking For?

Research into the desires of our youngest generations is similar, but the Springtide Research Group found that they are looking for opportunities to explore faith that support curiosity and flexibility and that are diverse and "unbundled," meaning they want the autonomy to pick and choose the activities or groups that mean the most to them.[72]

When I (Rachel) started forming a faith community for young adults in Phoenix two years ago, we had four key elements: hiking, cooking meals together, in-person worship, and volunteering in the community. I discovered that the Gen Zers would find their own rhythm of faith formation that included some or all of those elements each week. Our youngest emerging adults do not want to listen to sermons that remove all doubt or mystery from faith. While aspects of a black-and-white mentality might appeal to them initially (look at the rise of the "tradwife" role on social media), they want a faith that is flexible to grow with them

---

[72] https://springtideresearch.org/research/the-state-of-religion-2021.

and their needs. We might be quick to judge this generation for their exorbitant expectations, but what they want is similar to what formed the early church: a community that ate, worshiped, studied, and prayed together. They do not just want Sunday morning worship gatherings; they want a community where they can belong and grow in their faith alongside a group of young adults.

Recently, I (Rachel) stayed up until the early morning hours eating delicious pizza in Chicago and talking to two young women from Generation Z who had just returned from Lollapalooza, the annual four-day music festival. We talked about why they are not drawn to church anymore (even though one is a pastor's kid) and what might interest them. They echoed some of what we mentioned before: the church does not value the same things they do, and they cannot trust the church to act like Jesus. One of them, Taylor, mentioned that when she hears someone is a Christian, it is a red flag in her mind until that individual proves they are not "that" kind of Christian. She wants to make sure they are not a fundamentalist Christian whose faith or church causes harm to others. But both Taylor and her younger cousin agreed that *if* churches could use social media in authentic, genuine ways to let the world know they are different from the stereotypical church and *if* they offered a diverse, intergenerational community where they could find belonging, they would go.

While these young adults were not interested in an online-only faith community, they were curious about what it might look like to have a podcast with various voices and topics related to faith, a type of experience where they could listen and have pop-up parties with the podcast hosts and guests to go deeper and engage in discussion about the topics with others. Church is changing, but our need to belong and feel accepted by others is still the anchor of our ministry.

Jax (they/them) grew up in Pennsylvania but recently relocated to the West. When I asked this twenty-five-year-old about their church experience, they shared:

> When I was growing up, I was kind of roped into the whole church thing because it was a way that we could spend those hours together as a family. I sat there every week really just in it for the music because the worship band was awesome. This church was called Cornerstone, and the people there were like family to me. Even if I didn't believe in what was being talked about in the sermon, I believe in people.

Jax went on to share that they ended up leaving the church when it no longer felt like family, but they recently connected to a church that was transforming the community. This creative faith community helped them reconnect with God and their faith.

So What Can the Local Church Do?

If your church is looking for ways to create belonging for younger generations, here are some suggestions for next steps:

1. **De-center the stage**. When thinking about worship, discipleship, and fellowship, how can you create more equitable spaces where the pastors and leaders are not talking down to others but are talking with the community? How can you add more dialogue or discussion to your church activities in a non-threatening way? A slight caveat for this principle is that some young adults still long for a "rush" of emotion or a worship experience that feels more like a rock concert than routine worship. These young adults will not like this principle. They may want the stage in the center and to feel like they are

accessing a popular "brand" or influencer by being near the room's focal point. If your Sunday mornings include strobe lights and gifted musicians, utilize that as a strength. But it is important to mindfully engage in conversation and relational discipleship with young adults to form disciples and Christians, not simply consumers.

2. **Talk about what really matters**. Emerging adults do not want to fully engage in the life of a church until they know that the church is not afraid to take a stand on important issues. For instance, tell them you support Black Lives Matter. Show them you care about LGBTQIA+ liberation. Tell them that you, too, are concerned about climate change, rising mental health issues, or having rights that protect anyone who feels marginalized or unsafe. I (Kris) commonly engage in honest conversations that help equip my faith community to thoughtfully engage with God and their real-life experiences. We have discussed relevant topics such as racism, sexuality, gender diversity, faithful sexual practices, recreational drug use, loneliness, climate, etc., openly and thoughtfully (leading people to love God and to do no harm in their lives). I seek to be mindful of what our young adults are navigating daily and how our Christian discipleship might give meaning, clarity, or purpose to their lived experiences.

A caveat here for clergy is you cannot say these things if you do not mean them. So, if you do not share in the values of the young adults in your community, find ways to listen and learn from them and seek God's wisdom on your current stance and its unintended consequences.

I (Rachel) was raised by conservative Christian parents who

were ordained pastors in the United Methodist and American Baptist churches. When it came to the issue of homosexuality, they taught me to read scripture through a "literal" lens, and when I entered the ministry in my early twenties, I still held to their conservative views of scripture. While my parents were not affirming of the LGBTQIA+ community, they were very supportive of my call into ministry as a woman. When I would tell them about fellow pastors or speakers who called me an abomination for being a female pastor, they told me not to be defensive towards the naysayers but to simply ask, "Do you see the Holy Spirit at work in my ministry? Do you see spiritual growth happening? Is there fruit here that is evident of God's presence? If so, then how could God move through me and this ministry if I'm an abomination?"

I served as a church planter in a faith community that grew from ten young adults in 2009 to over 250 people involved in weekly worship within a decade (while I was a nursing mom of two young children with a husband who served a different church on the other side of town). So, it was evident the Holy Spirit was moving in this community, and as the planting pastor, I had a part in God's work in this place.

So, I applied the same principle to church planters I met from the queer community. I saw them faithfully and openly loving God and being who God created them to be, and their churches were flourishing and transforming the surrounding community in life-giving, powerful ways. How could I deny that God was at work in and through them? Some of the most humble, faithful, and gifted laity in my church were couples from the LGBTQIA+ community. How could I deny who God had called them to be?

As a female pastor, I empathize with queer clergy colleagues who feel marginalized or judged by conservative Christians. This empathy led me on a journey to read through the scriptures in the original languages, which helped me see that my interpretation of the passages on homosexuality was steeped more in my own culture than in the culture in which it was written.

Some of the theology imparted to me from childhood was not only biblically inaccurate, but it was also harmful. I needed to be intentional about how I employed my lived experience with the living Word of God to truly be a follower of Christ. If I had not taken time to listen to God, my community, and the wisdom of my parents, which led me to a very different theological position, then I would not be the pastor I am today. When the black Bishop of the Virginia Conference asked clergy to go to the Charlottesville riot to offer a counterwitness to racism, discrimination, and hatred, I accepted. And it made me a better pastor. When a lesbian couple in my church asked me to join the Women's March because they needed spiritual support, I accepted. And it made me a better pastor. When the increasingly racially diverse and queer-affirming Western jurisdiction asked me to leave my predominantly white, male, national agency position to witness how the Holy Spirit was moving, I accepted. And it made me a better pastor. When we share in the social justice concerns of young adults, it builds a bridge for deeper belonging and community as we sojourn together until "justice rolls down like waters and righteousness like an ever flowing stream."[73]

---

[73] Amos 5:24.

3. **Inspire and engage your leaders.** Australian
    sociologist Mark McCrindle notes that while older
    generations were accustomed to leadership styles that
    were more controlling, directive, and coordinating,
    younger generations want leaders to guide, empower,
    and inspire them. We need to shift from the top-down
    managerial/CEO style of leadership in the church to
    one that is more holistic and relational.

4. **Actively support your young adult leaders.**
    When we have young adults in leadership, create
    systems where you check in with them to support
    and encourage them so they feel inspired to
    continue the work. Young adults crave relationships
    and intergenerational mentorship in loving and
    respectful ways. Take them out for coffee once a
    month to thank them for what they are doing. Ask
    them what they are doing well, what questions
    they have, and how you can support them in their
    journey. Knowing that you care about them for
    more than their leadership contributions will
    speak volumes and keep them from feeling like a
    commodity in the church.

5. **Prepare the community for conflict, which
    can build trust and vulnerability if handled
    correctly.** Young adults have a diversity of thought
    and are not always conflict-averse, so find ways
    to handle disagreements in the community that
    are healthy so younger generations do not simply
    "block" or "ghost" you and move on to another group
    of people. Use conflict as a way to build trust. Find
    ways to engage in healing circles or conflict circles
    where young adults are invited to listen to others
    and feel heard. Do not steer away from conflict or
    see it as a negative thing. Instead, it can be used
    as a way to build a bridge between people who are
    experiencing cultural differences in some way. We

would like to remind our politically minded friends that if George Bush AND Hillary Clinton can both be members of United Methodist churches, then we can find a way to get along, too.[74]

6. **Belonging requires boundaries.** When I (Rachel) was in seminary at Duke Divinity School, I heard Stanley Hauerwas refer to pastors as "quivering masses of availability." The research giant Barna has started a resilient pastor initiative in response to surprising research that finds that younger clergy and female clergy are at the greatest risk of burning out and leaving the ministry. Only 35 percent of pastors under forty-five consider themselves "very satisfied" with their job in the church, a number which increases to 58 percent for clergy over forty-five years old.[75] In addition, while most male clergy still feel confident about their call to ministry (52 percent), that number drops to less than half (42 percent) when they surveyed female clergy.

The reality is that all clergy are struggling as the percentage of clergy who have seriously considered quitting ministry has increased by almost 400 percent in less than ten years, with 40 percent of clergy saying they have considered walking away. Pastors and clergy struggle to have healthy boundaries in the life of the church.

There is one word Christians love to use to describe themselves that was never used to describe Jesus Christ. Do you know what that word is? "NICE." Just because we follow Jesus does not mean we are "nice" people. We are not called to be nice. We are called to be loving. We love God, others, and

---

[74] https://www.tampabay.com/archive/2001/01/20/bush-is-nation-s-third-methodist-president/ https://time.com/2927925/hillary-clintons-religion/.

[75] https://www.barna.com/research/pastoral-security-confidence/.

ourselves by setting healthy boundaries for what we can and cannot do and who we can and cannot be. Communicating those boundaries effectively to others can be the start of a beautiful community of belonging because we know what we can and cannot do, where we can help, and what can harm us. In this, we are protecting and renewing ourselves for the demands of pastoral ministry.

Through self-care practices for clergy, we have the emotional and spiritual capacity to co-create and cultivate communities that foster belonging and spiritual connection. We are not simply uplifting and maintaining an institution; we are giving life to a church community centered on people and belonging.

CHAPTER ELEVEN

Safe Digital Spaces
that Foster Belonging

This is a hard chapter for us to write. Because younger generations are digital natives drawn to apps and online content on a daily basis, we know churches need to catch up to culture and foster a strong and healthy online presence. One of the main reasons the church is in decline today could be that we did not follow in the footsteps of John Wesley and George Whitfield, who went out into the fields of England in the 1700s to be with the people. While John Wesley was not initially a fan of leaving the walls of the church to share God's Word with others, he started "field preaching" regularly when he saw its effectiveness. In his journal from April of 1739, he states:

> At four in the afternoon, I submitted to be more vile and proclaimed in the highways the glad tidings of salvation, speaking from a little eminence in a ground adjoining to the city, to about three thousand people. The Scripture on which I spoke was this ... "The Spirit of the Lord is upon me, because he hath anointed me to preach the gospel to the poor; he hath sent me to heal the broken-hearted, to preach deliverance to the captives, and recovering of sight to the blind, to set at liberty them that are bruised, to proclaim the acceptable year of the Lord" Sunday, 8.—At seven in the morning I preached to about a thousand persons at Bristol, and afterward to about fifteen hundred on the top of Hannam Mount in Kingswood. ... About five thousand were in the afternoon at Rose Green (on the other side of Kingswood).

If John Wesley could reach thousands of people working outside the walls of the church over 250 years ago, then we can reach hundreds of thousands of young adults by going out into the *digital fields* where they spend their time. Gen Z has been heavily active online for over a decade, but most churches only started to take social media and an online presence seriously during the global pandemic.

If we want to reach young adults, we can do that in digital spaces. However, we also see research coming out about the rising mental health issues and struggles with eating disorders in our younger generations as they feel pressured to brand themselves like the beautiful people and things they see online. In fact, research shows the number of teens who experienced eating disorders more than doubled during the COVID-19 pandemic, and social media is a contributing factor.[76]

So, how do we create safe digital spaces that foster belonging? Should we move to online-only churches where we can engage with the church when our mental health is longing for connection instead of waiting for Sunday morning? Should we try out digital churches so we do not have to worry about our appearance because all the congregation sees is our avatar? Some pastors think we are already behind the curve on this and need to continue building community online. One of those trailblazers is Rev. Nathan Webb, pastor of Checkpoint Church in North Carolina. Nathan was kind enough to write a thorough explanation of what it looks like to create community and belonging in online-only platforms like Twitch, YouTube, and Discord. We are mindful that the majority of our churches are not equipped or necessarily called to move to an online-only

---

[76] https://www.umassmed.edu/news/news-archives/2023/03/eating-disorders-in-teens-more-than-doubled-during-pandemic/.

platform, especially in smaller and rural communities without high-speed Internet or with no Internet access at all. What might be the middle ground for us?

We will share five main principles and then five main platforms that might help you develop a strategy.

Five Main Principles for Reaching Younger Generations:

1. **Know your "who" and "why" before looking at your "what" and "how."** I (Rachel) consulted with a church that really wanted to connect with teenagers, but they were trying to do it by focusing solely on their Facebook posts. Pew Research in 2023 noted that the number of teens using Facebook decreased from 71 percent in 2013-2014 to 32 percent in 2022. Out of those 32 percent of teens on Facebook, only 3 percent of them report using Facebook on a regular basis.[77] However, Facebook or Instagram can be a great way to meet Millennial parents looking for community, while TikTok and YouTube are better options for younger generations.

   The first step in utilizing social media to reach younger generations is to figure out *which* generation you want to reach first and *why* you want to reach them so you can figure out *what* to post. If your goal is to grow your social media following, then you might do more engaging posts or quizzes. However, if your goal is to invite people to your Christmas Eve service, then a targeted ad on Facebook or strategically sharing your online worship is a better use of your time and resources. Context matters. Who you are called to reach matters, so start with "who" and "why" before you move to "what" or "how."

---

[77] https://www.pewresearch.org/short-reads/2023/04/24/teens-and-social-media-key-findings-from-pew-research-center-surveys/.

2. **Establish a covenant or expectations for those who manage and participate on your social media platforms**. Sometimes, online pastors feel they must be present 24/7 for anyone who sends a Direct Message or reaches out in the middle of the night when they have existential questions. No pastor can work 24/7. Even God rested on the seventh day! Being clear about your boundaries and what the church leaders can expect from the congregation and vice versa is an important step in setting up healthy online expectations. It is also an easy way to put in some guidelines or language about how to protect minors or impressionable young adults from being groomed or targeted online in unhealthy or illegal ways.

3. **Encourage regular social media "detox," where participants turn off their phones and plan to meet in person to foster belonging.** The concept of a "social media detox" has grown in recent years, where participants unplug for three days to two weeks to experience the benefits of removing themselves from all social media platforms. A recent article published by Harvard shares the benefits of such a detox, including improved sleep, improved mental health, and decreased FOMO (Fear of Missing Out), among other benefits.[78] And depending on the age and online activity of your youth or young adult, you might want to look into their participation in online gaming. Alok Kanojia recently published *How to Raise a Healthy Gamer: End Power Struggles, Break Bad Screen Habits and Transform Your Relationship with Your Kids,* which also offers healthy suggestions for when and how to create healthy distance between technology and our teenagers.

---

[78] https://summer.harvard.edu/blog/need-a-break-from-social-media-heres-why-you-should-and-how-to-do-it/.

4. **Live into conjunctive theology in your online approach.** One reason we're United Methodist pastors is our love of John Wesley's conjunctive theology. He did not think that following Christ was all about faith *or* all about works. It was a "both/and," faith *and* works. Methodists do not believe in grace *or* accountability but in grace *and* works. Some churches want to be in digital spaces to offer content like podcasts, YouTube worship services, or one-minute TikTok monologues. Other churches want to be in digital spaces to form relationships and engage with their online community through Facebook groups, Zoom Bible studies, or Discord channels. When looking at ministry in digital spaces, consider a "both/and" approach to diversify your reach and discipleship opportunities.

5. **If it is not authentically you, it wastes your time**. If you think that sounding "mindful" or "demure" on a social media platform is all you need to attract young adults, then you are missing the point.[79] Because they are inundated with influencers online, they long for an unfiltered reality where they see who people really are and hear about how they really feel. Younger generations can spot churches or clergy trying to fake it, and it is a huge turnoff. *So be yourself!* What matters more than being perfect is being perfectly you. Honesty, authenticity, and relatability are key if you want to connect with emerging generations in online spaces.

---

[79] https://news.abs-cbn.com/lifestyle/2024/8/28/-very-demure-very-mindful-trend-takes-over-social-media-1600.

Five Main Platforms to Consider for Younger Generations:

1. **To reach Millennials and Gen X, focus on Facebook and cross-post to Instagram.** We do not recommend posting cheesy memes. Instead, find meaningful, engaging content that encourages interaction with people through liking, sharing, or commenting on your post. Creating Facebook groups can be a powerful way to curate a sense of belonging in an online space.

2. **To reach Gen Z and Gen Alpha (and even some Millennials), TikTok or Instagram reels can help you show your brand in authentic and impactful ways.** Do not heavily edit your content. Keep it short, creative, and authentically you.

3. **Do not underestimate the power of a text message.** If you have young adults in worship and you want to send out a group text to all of them to thank them for being in worship or tell them how awesome they are or when the next gathering is, do not be afraid to utilize group texting! While it might drive some Millennials crazy, it is a common form of communication for those in college or young adulthood.

   A meaningful way in which I (Kris) connect and engage with young adults in the life of The Journey is through text messages. Each week, I think of a few people I want to intentionally encourage, pray for, or check in on to make sure all is well in their world. In a predominately young congregation, pastoral care looks more like text messages of encouragement and checking in than home or hospital visits.

4. **Consider podcasts in addition to YouTube for publishing sermons or dialogues about faith with**

younger generations so they can access your content "on the go." According to Pew Research, two-thirds of young adults ages eighteen to twenty-nine have listened to a podcast in the last year. The church has a huge opportunity to publish its content on the go. Podcasts are becoming increasingly common, so get in those spaces and find ways to market your content and dialogues so others can find it.[80]

During the pandemic, after launching The Journey Church less than one year before, it became clear I (Kris) could not simply wait until things may one day return to "normal" to innovate and live out our vision. We boldly decided to do whatever it takes to connect new people to Jesus in a digital age.

Expert Opinion, a weekly community conversation series, became our first bold decision. This conversation series became a platform for community leaders, local theologians, counselors, professionals, nonprofit leaders, and local experts to share how they understood the unique season of 2020. We launched this Sunday evening conversation series to create a space where our current members and city could engage in relevant conversations and listen to various experts share their understanding of what was happening during the pandemic. In a season where many are questioning the relevance of church and the Christian faith, we wanted to create a non-Sunday morning space to host honest conversations about what is happening in our local area and our global world. We did not merely want to survive the new reality of church in a global pandemic; we were convinced we could thrive and

---

80 https://www.pewresearch.org/journalism/2023/04/18/podcast-use-among-different-age-groups/#:~:text=Younger percent20adults percent20in percent20the percent20United,elders percent20to percent20engage percent20with percent20podcasts.

create a space for sincere life-giving conversation and community via the digital platform.

5. **Websites should not require content that needs to be changed daily or weekly** (other than updating your calendar or sermon/YouTube links). Think of your website as a billboard. Use evergreen[81] content and Linktree[82] on social media to drive traffic to your homepage.

The digital space, including church websites, should be oriented around connection: connecting people to others in the digital space and ultimately connecting us all to God. Through the faithful work of engaging thoughtfully with the digital space, we can create conditions for younger adults to experience belonging and the liberation of Jesus Christ. It is worth noting, though, as Dr. King once remarked, "We have allowed our technology to outdistance our theology and for this reason we find ourselves caught up with many problems."[83] As churches lean further into digital ministry, we want our theology to continue to shape and form our personal and corporate relationships with technology, keeping the love of God and the love of people at the center of our digital practices while, at the same time, helping young adults manage the dangers online.

---

[81] Here's a great resource to explain what evergreen content is. Basically, it's content that doesn't have to change because it's not time sensitive. It consistently shares important information that's relevant to those trying to learn more about you but doesn't require a lot of time to continually update and change. https://digitalmarketinginstitute.com/blog/the-beginners-guide-to-evergreen-content.

[82] Linktree is like a mini website that has links to all of your important social media platforms to help people connect to you quickly in countless ways: https://www.methodmarketing.org/blog/what-is-linktree/.

[83] https://www.nobelprize.org/prizes/peace/1964/king/lecture/.

CHAPTER TWELVE

Listen and Love, Don't Judge and Nag

In a quick conversation with any young adult today, we find that many feel a deep sense of uncertainty, shame, and insecurity. As we seek to understand further and engage with followers under 40, we must shift our approach. The church's traditional focus on sin and guilt is no longer compelling for young adults. Young adults will not flock to hear sermons about "Sinners in the Hands of an Angry God" as they did for Jonathan Edwards in the 1740s. Younger generations are already navigating a world filled with significant insecurity, often enlarged by the rise of technology and social media. What has worked in previous generations—a faith centered on guilt, sin, and the threat of hell—will not work anymore. Younger generations are not looking for judgment or nagging. They are looking for something positive, redeeming, and healing. Simply put, they are looking for a church with a culture and practices of listening and love.

The Deep Insecurity in Younger Generations

We celebrate the technological advances in society. I (Kris) have my cell phone or computer near me most of the time. I appreciate the sense of connection that is always virtually with me. Technological advances have brought incredible advantages and enjoyment to many. And yet, this new digital and technological age has also brought adverse feelings. Due to peer pressure experienced with technology, there is a growing sense of inadequacy and insecurity. New dynamics are at play: constant comparisons, cyberbullying, and a sense of pressure to create and curate a perfect life online. The American Psychological Association has found that 90 percent of Gen Z experience stress and anxiety related to their unique social media and technology usage.[84] The pressure to embody a perfect online persona to peers contributes to significant anxiety, self-doubt, and constant comparison.

So, imagine a young adult arriving to worship on a Sunday morning and hearing a message of guilt and shame centered on personal sin. Instead of being inspired to confess and draw closer to Jesus and the church, they recoil into their feelings of guilt and shame. Their insecurities are inflamed. These insecurities and anxiety imposed by a digital age make it ever so important for the church and clergy to rethink ministry practices.

In particular, to help young adults feel valued, accepted, known, and loved, Christian leaders today must create spaces for young adults to grapple with their identity in safety. Instead of focusing on bad news (i.e., guilt, shame), what if we create environments and communities centered on hope, healing, love, and acceptance? What if we reclaim salvation through the lens of healing the cosmos? We do this not only to be relevant but also to be hope-filled and to help heal the

---

[84] American Psychological Association, "Stress in America: Generation Z," 2018.

brokenness in the world. The church should be a place (and people) where young adults find support, peace, and solace, not further judgment, comparison, or condemnation.

A Culture of Listening and Love

Jesus' very life and approach to teaching were oriented around this practice of listening and loving rather than judging and nagging. In John 13:34-35, Jesus commands, "A new command I give you: Love one another. As I have loved you, so you must love one another. By this, everyone will know that you are my disciples, if you love one another." Love is the hallmark of true discipleship.

If love is the command that should orient and lead every aspect of the Christian community, then these profound words of theologian Henri Nouwen speak to how we do this: Nouwen once said, "Listening is much more than allowing another to talk while waiting for a chance to respond. Listening is paying full attention to others and welcoming them into our very being."[85]

Christian community facilitates significant time to think, speak, and listen. And yet, Nouwen deepens our understanding of listening. Listening is not simply hearing the facts and details of one's sharing; it is a profoundly different kind of deep and attentive listening—a type of listening where one can be heard, understood, and loved without conditions or expectations. This very type of listening is what is yearned for today. Emerging adults do not simply want to be mentored by others; they want to benefit from deep personal listening.

---

[85] Henri J.M. Nouwen, *Life of the Beloved: Spiritual Living in a Secular World* (Crossroad, 1992).

The Psychological Harm of Judgment

If there is a deep desire to be heard, understood, and loved without conditions, then we must realize that judgment and nagging have the potential to cause significant psychological effects. Feelings of shame, inadequacy, and alienation can all stem from the effects of judgment and nagging. No one likes being criticized, excluded, or judged, and these messages are often internalized. When someone experiences constant criticism and judgment by persons of power—such as clergy— these messages can potentially harm that person's mental and emotional well-being. In an attempt to "save" someone, these internalized messages produce harm and lower their self-concept. It is no wonder, then, that young adults are quickly leaving these places of detrimental messaging and communities of psychological harm.

The Australian psychologist Nick Haslam identifies this same concern about expanding the term "safety." Haslam states, "For most of the 20th century, the word 'safety' referred almost exclusively to physical safety. Only in the late 1980s did the term 'emotional safety' appear at more than trace levels in Google's Ngram viewer. From 1985 to 2010, at the start of the Great Rewiring, the term's frequency rose rapidly and steadily, a 600 percent increase."[86] There is a clear awareness and sensitivity around the emotional safety of our children and adults alike. In our modern era, safety is no longer limited to someone's physical self but a desire to maintain and steward one's emotional self, too.

Jesus teaches and warns us against judgmentalism at

---

[86] Haidt, Jonathan, The Anxious Generation: How the Great Rewiring of Childhood Is Causing an Epidemic of Mental Illness (Penguin Press, 2024).

the foundation of our shared faith. Jesus clearly states in Matthew 7:1-5:

> *Do not judge, or you too will be judged. For in the same way you judge others, you will be judged, and with the measure you use, it will be measured to you. Why do you look at the speck of sawdust in your brother's eye and pay no attention to the plank in your own eye? How can you say to your brother, "Let me take the speck out of your eye," when all the time there is a plank in your own eye? You hypocrite, first take the plank out of your own eye, and then you will see clearly to remove the speck from your brother's eye.*

Here, like in the rest of the Sermon on the Mount, Jesus is not offering advice for success in the relationships of this world. Instead, Jesus is calling us to live in the light of God's dawning Kindom. On earth, people judge and criticize all the time. But in God's Kindom, in God's space and place, in the presence of love for the divine, people do not judge. Instead, they go above and beyond to love others well. The relevant, meaningful Christian community of the future is a community that centers on the compassion and grace of Jesus.

Aidan's Story

Aidan's story is a heartbreaking example showing the consequences of judgment and lack of understanding within the church. Growing up as a pastor's son in the Wesleyan Church during the height of the conservative evangelical movement in the 1990s, Aidan was surrounded by a community that felt like family. His life revolved around the church where his father served as the pastor, continuing the legacy of his grandfather, who had also pastored the same church. Everyone expected Aidan to follow in their footsteps— everyone except Aidan.

From a young age, Aidan knew he was different. By the time he was a teenager, Aidan realized he was gay, but in his insular environment, he had no examples of what it meant to be gay. The only thing he knew about being gay came from the church, where he was taught to fear and be ashamed of his identity. The "clobber passages" of the Bible, often used to condemn LGBTQIA+ individuals, weighed heavily on him. At fourteen, Aidan attempted to take his own life and was sent to conversion therapy, where he was subjected to invasive and humiliating sessions with a NARTH[87] therapist. When he was seventeen, the minister of music's wife attempted to "cast the demon of homosexuality" out of him, further deepening his shame and isolation.

Despite trying to suppress his true self, Aidan could not escape who he was. His experiences at a Wesleyan college were just as shaming, as he was placed on probation after it was discovered he was gay, resulting in the painful realization for Aidan that there was no place in the Wesleyan church as he was. The relentless judgment and pressure to change drove him away from the church entirely. Today, over twenty years later, Aidan has restored his relationship with his family, who are now kind and loving toward him and his partner. However, he no longer believes in God and has not attended church regularly since college. Aidan sometimes wonders if his faith might have survived had he grown up in a more affirming church, one that prioritized love and understanding over rigid doctrine and judgment.

Aidan's story is a sobering reminder of the damage that can be done when the church fails to love and listen, choosing instead to judge and nag those who do not fit its perceived mold.

---

[87] National Association for Research & Therapy of Homosexuality.

Practices of Harm in the Church

Specific practices in some churches have caused harm to people in the Christian community, for instance, moments of public shaming when someone has been publicly called out for their sins during public worship services or community gatherings. Sadly, I (Kris) recall hearing a story once that a person was called out for being gay in a worship service, leading to the church elders having a "prayer" moment over this individual. Harm. A clear moment of shame. But it has not always been as evident—like when a certain group or individuals are excluded from church activities or membership based on race, sexuality, gender, or ideological perspective. Often, these exclusions are based on identity or past actions and seek to maintain the "purity" of a community. Those who are often excluded are not persons in the majority of society. In an attempt to maintain this level of "purity," we quickly forget the compelling words of Jesus that call us to love.

Two additional practices of harm in the church center on conditional love and rigid doctrines. When a faith community simply dictates and enforces strict conditions focused on theology, scripture, or doctrines, it leaves no room for questions, doubts, or diverse perspectives. Also, only fully accepting or supporting those who conform to the community's dogmatic standards leaves no room for the beautiful diversity and creativity that is God. These practices create environments of fear and judgment, driving people away rather than drawing them closer to God.

Practices of Love and Peace

Instead, we imagine a world where more loving, inclusive communities emerge and forgiveness, acceptance, and peace are experienced.

- **Forgiveness and Reconciliation**: Centering a community on the foundational element of forgiveness and reconciliation in *all* relationships.

- **Unconditional Love**: Demonstrating God's unconditional love by accepting individuals as they are without requiring them to meet certain conditions.

- **Supportive Listening**: Creating environments where people can share their struggles and stories without fear of judgment and where we practice the level of listening Nouwen encourages.

- **Grace-filled Language and Welcome**. Each week at The Journey, one of our leaders stands up and proclaims a bold word of inclusion and welcome. We make it clear that no matter whom someone loves, how they identify, what they were doing the night before or plan to do again tonight, where they live, or the color of their skin, they are boldly and fully welcome at The Journey. We even give our first-time guests t-shirts that proclaim, "We All Belong," with our welcome statement on the back.[88] To foster love and listening, we must declare the type of culture and environment we are setting as we host our communal practices.

---

[88] Welcome statement: "The Journey Church is a life-giving, multi-ethnic, and inclusive church in urban Harrisburg, PA, where our desire is to help people find belonging, experience the liberative spirit of Jesus, seek justice in the world, and radically love our neighbors (aka our vision).

As a faith community, The Journey welcomes and honors people of all ethnicities, gender identities, sexual orientations, religious backgrounds, ages, perspectives, economic or immigrant status, as beloved by God and of equal worth and dignity."

- **Promoting Peace**: Engaging in peacemaking activities within the church and the broader community. For example, I (Kris) co-hosted a peace pilgrimage in our city with an intentional interfaith worship experience highlighting the stories and trauma of our Palestinian siblings. I (Rachel) helped kids from a local United Methodist church organize a Black Lives Matter protest for families, and we met with the local sheriff to get his permission to hold the event outside of their building. The sheriffs arrived with popsicles to join us in the protest following the senseless murder of George Floyd.

Moving Forward with Love

As we strive to engage younger generations deeper with Jesus and the church, we must lead our church toward a culture of listening and love. Let us move beyond judgment and nagging to a place of acceptance and support. Let us live out our values consistently, build tables—not walls—and embrace a theology of inclusivity. In the words of Latine theologian Miguel A. De La Torre, "Our task is to reflect God's love in such a way that no one feels excluded from the table of grace."[89] This is our calling as followers of Jesus. As we connect with more young adults in our communities, this is our opportunity to embody a church where *all* can find belonging, hope, and love.

---

[89] Miguel A. De La Torre, *Embracing Hopelessness* (Fortress Press, 2017).

CHAPTER THIRTEEN

Reclaim Spiritual Disciplines

COVID-19 showed us that we are doing a horrible job of caring for ourselves. Having a season with more margin and time at home helped our society come face-to-face with the reality that we feel overworked, overwhelmed, over-scheduled, and ill-prepared to do anything about it. I (Rachel) was on a Zoom call last week with a diverse group of new church start pastors from three states, and we were talking about our lack of self-care practices. Two participants stood out from the group as having a healthy balance between work and rest, incorporating daily rhythms into their lives for rest and renewal. One pastor in Sedona, Arizona, wakes up every morning to hike with the accountability and help of a friend who meets her each morning. Another Tongan pastor in Tucson, Arizona, helps coach a local high school football team and finds renewal in doing something completely different from what church life demands from him.

When it comes to emerging generations, they also feel overwhelmed and exhausted a lot of the time. As church leaders, we often assume that what younger generations are looking for is something light-hearted that will not require a lot of time, energy, or commitment. That assumption is wrong. If young adults are going to invest in something or a particular community, they want it to feel worthy of the cause, and they want it to change their lives. This desire to find deep belonging through rites and rituals over time is not new to society. Psychologist David DeSteno's 2021 book, *How God Works: The Science Behind the Benefits of Religion,* notes that when we engage in spiritual practices, we focus less on ourselves and build trust with a larger community, which leads to improved well-being.[90]

Dietrich Bonhoeffer was a spiritual leader during World War II who died in a concentration camp. He once said:

> *Cheap grace is the preaching of forgiveness without requiring repentance, baptism without church discipline, communion without confession, absolution without personal confession. Cheap grace is grace without discipleship, grace without the cross, grace without Jesus living and incarnate. Costly grace is the gospel which must be sought again and again. The gift which must be asked for, the door at which a man must knock. Such grace is costly because it calls us to follow and it is grace because it calls us to follow Jesus Christ. It is costly because it costs a man his life and it is grace because it gives a man the only true life.[91]*

Many churches are failing to reach younger generations today because they assume that what they want is a watered-down faith or low expectations for what it means to follow Christ. In fact, younger generations crave a reclamation of the spiritual disciplines that they have not seen their parents or grandparents living out. These spiritual disciplines seem to be so much more life-giving to them than what the world

---

90 David DeSteno, *How God Works: The Science Behind the Benefits of Religion* (Simon & Schuster, 2021).

91 Dietrich Bonhoeffer, *The Cost of Discipleship, rev. ed.* (Macmillan Publishing Company, 1963).

offers. They want resources for how to find balance and calm, strength and resilience, accountability, and connection to the world around them.

Fifteen years ago, when I (Rachel) was starting a church where the majority of our congregants were under forty-five, the most popular small group we had was based on *Celebration of Discipline* by Richard Foster, which teaches the spiritual disciplines of meditation, prayer, fasting, study, simplicity, solitude, submission, service, confession, worship, guidance and celebration.[92] So how can we contextualize some of the disciplines Foster espoused for our younger generations?

Meditation and Prayer with Younger Generations

Many young adults are open to meditation because they hear about the scientific benefits[93] and see it utilized by all five major faith traditions: Hinduism, Buddhism, Judaism, Christianity, and Islam. Apps like Headspace and Insite Timer offer free meditation classes that may or may not be faith-based or Christian in context. Reverend Heather Rodrigues is a United Methodist pastor of a church in Durham, North Carolina, and one of their most popular community events in recent years has been a sound bath that they host in the sanctuary as a way of bridging the spiritual discipline of meditation with their faith community.[94]

---

[92] Richard Foster, *Celebration of Discipline: The Path to Spiritual Growth* (Hodder & Stoughton, 2008).

[93] https://health.ucdavis.edu/blog/cultivating-health/10-health-benefits-of-meditation-and-how-to-focus-on-mindfulness-and-compassion/2022/12.

[94] A sound bath is when your body is "bathed" in sound waves (often using singing bowls) to help soothe your body with the vibrations and sound- https://health.clevelandclinic.org/sound-bath.

Meditation and different forms of prayer should be incorporated into all aspects of faith formation in your church: for example, writing out prayers or texting them to a Google phone number, trying tongsung kido,[95] and incorporating illustrated artwork into prayer times where people pray by coloring to express their feelings. There are unlimited options for adapting the importance of prayer and meditation to meet the spiritual needs of young adults.

Fasting, Simplicity, and Submission for Younger Generations

More than any of the others, the spiritual disciplines of fasting, simplicity, and submission can be triggering for younger generations. With the increase in mental health issues and eating disorders among younger generations and scientific data showing an increase in eating disorders for youth and young adults who engage in intermittent fasting,[96] it is crucial to consider different approaches to the principle behind this spiritual discipline.

Fasting from food is a way of denying ourselves something we need to survive so we can learn to hunger and thirst for God and turn to more spiritual ways of being. For young adults today who are drawn to deny themselves food for different reasons, it is important to adapt the theological principle for younger generations. What is it that we can deny ourselves so we can learn how to hunger and thirst for God

---

[95] https://caac.ptsem.edu/a-prayer-that-breaks-the-silence-tongsung-kido-and-the-holy-spirits-humanizing-work/.

[96] https://pubmed.ncbi.nlm.nih.gov/36368052/.

and experience more spiritual ways of being? Perhaps it is the social media detox we referenced earlier, fasting from self-criticism, or fasting from spending money on things that support or promote the value of an external image over an internal one. When it comes to fasting, we must know our audience and then teach and model this discipline so young adults can build a closer connection to God and experience greater healing in their lives.

Similarly, when it comes to simplicity, it can be a hard sell to younger generations. Because the overwhelming amount of social media influence tells them that the signs of happiness are wealth and a privileged lifestyle, they can believe that simplicity is a negative attribute, not a positive one. In other situations, they are so inundated with digital messaging that living on a farm and embracing a simple, low-tech approach to life can seem appealing or entertaining, but they don't really know what it looks like to live an "off-line" life. Teaching and modeling for them how to embrace simple practices, grounding techniques, or principles for living lives of purpose can be very compelling and encouraging for younger generations.

The issue of submission is a hot topic for many Millennials and Gen Zers who were raised in conservative homes, taught that abusive or patriarchal systems were biblical, and were instructed and demanded to subscribe to a literal interpretation of Ephesians 5. We remind our congregations that Ephesians 5 was radical in its day, not for its talk of wives submitting to their husbands, but for the command that husbands love their wives like Christ loves the church. In that day and time, husbands were expected to love their wives like they would a piece of property or something they owned that could be treated however they liked. But Christ was willing to die for the church, and any man who is not willing to die for his wife, sacrificing everything for her health and well-being, is not worth submitting to. Christ died for the church so we would not have to die at the hands of selfish and sinful abusers.

More and more, emerging adult Christians are becoming exvangelicals because they see conservative churches forcing women and children into a place of harm to satiate the male aggressors who seek to exert power and do not love their families "well." Submission should be taught as *mutual* submission, where we can put the needs of others above our own needs. We are able to mutually submit because we know we're in a healthy environment where we all want a shared goal or common good, and it's life-giving to say no to yourself for a larger purpose. We need to redefine "submission" to heal the church moving forward.

Study and Service for Younger Generations

When it comes to study and service for younger generations, one word matters: "engagement." These emerging adults do not want to sit and listen to a lecture. They want to talk about it, text about it, push back on the concepts, and lean more deeply into curiosity and questions. Do not have a Bible study or youth worship service that does not give them a space to engage with what they are hearing or seeing. Give them a role to play. Similarly, when it comes to service, think of relational ways to engage the community instead of transactional ones. Young adults do not want to just collect money for a local service project. They want to get out and build a ramp, show up with signs at a protest, or get signatures to add a justice-related issue to the ballot.

One of my (Rachel) favorite scripture verses is John 1:14, where we read, "The Word became flesh and dwelt among us." Eugene Peterson's translation of that verse in The Message says, "The Word became flesh and blood and moved into the neighborhood." When we offer study and service opportunities that engage the hearts, heads, and hands of young adults, we are shaping followers of Christ who are Christ's presence in the neighborhood. They are living out the word of God through their actions, and that will transform not just the surrounding community but the faith community as well.

Solitude and Guidance for Younger Generations

Young adults are very curious and open to exploring what these disciplines truly mean, how to practice them, and how to curate a rule of life that grounds them when the waves come crashing in. Last year, I (Rachel) signed up for a short-term study on "letting go," hosted by The Nearness. I paid around 150 dollars for this eight-week study on Zoom which was frightening and refreshing at the same time. The group had no official leader (decentralized power structures!), and we took turns each week fulfilling the role of timekeeper and reader between the six of us.

I learned alongside young adults logging in from Kansas to Australia with a Ukrainian dad joining the group. As we spoke openly and freely through the structured discussion points each week, we built individualized rituals that could help us forgive others, God, or ourselves. This small group replaced church for many of the young adults in the group who felt like the honest discussion and traditions they experienced in that online setting were more profound than any faith formation they experienced in a pew on Sunday mornings.

So how do we create "Nearness" experiences in our communities? You might begin by joining a Nearness study[97] or some kind of online gathering where you are the guest: your goal is to listen, learn, and love the people in the space. Then look at your local context (physically or digitally) and determine how you can offer spaces of solitude and guidance that feel both organic and intentional.

Worship, Service, and Celebration for Younger Generations

How are churches fostering worship, service, and celebration in a practical way? There is a Methodist church in Germany that does "semester church," where people meet weekly for four to six weeks and then take a month off so they learn to practice the rhythms of Sabbath and create more time for their small groups, which are ongoing and offer more relational discipleship. The Korean Methodist Church has a very structured system of providing biblical teaching and prayer services for new(er) Christians, and that also creates mentorship systems where anyone can find someone to help them grow in their faith on a regular basis.

When I (Rachel) spent a year starting a missional community in Phoenix, we were not in a church on Sundays, although we made it a goal to worship online or in person at least once a month. We spent time eating meals, hiking, volunteering, or

---

[97] https://www.nearness.coop.

showing up at protests in the community so these young adults could see faith lived out throughout the week.

For me (Kris), we create rhythms throughout the year that foster a greater sense of sabbath and living out worship. For example, every Sunday after Christmas, we shift our worship experience solely online to foster rest and renewal for all volunteers and church members. This practice began a few years ago when New Year's Day was on a Sunday. I quickly realized that many of our congregation members would spend time with friends the night before. So, to still invest in the spiritual life of our church (while being realistic about this particular Sunday), we moved the service online and prerecorded a worship experience. This practice has become a beautiful rhythm to our holiday celebrations.

If you are in a local church that is trying to reach young adults, do not be afraid to make some changes in your order of worship on Sundays. Bring back a more intentional time of confession or make celebration a bigger deal at the communion table. Find ways to teach or explain not just what you are doing but *why* you are doing a spiritual practice and witness the impact it can have if you continue to practice these principles every day of the week. The first name for Christians in scripture was actually "followers of the Way." Young adults today do not want a faith that stops at the sanctuary doors. They want to know about this way of living that can change everything for them and the world around them. Will we engage in spiritual practices that can provide the scaffolding young adults need to grow in their discipleship and centering in a complex world?

CHAPTER FOURTEEN

Closing

As we come to the end of *Followers Under 40,* **it is abundantly clear** that the challenges facing the church today are quite profound. And yet, baked within these challenges also lies a beautiful, holy, and sacred opportunity before us. We are invited to lead and embody a church that can evolve and adapt to become a place of deep hope, healing, and transformation for the new and emerging generations.

We have sought to offer a clear and compelling picture of the current realities: declining attendance, aging congregations, and the significant (and painful) disconnect between the church practices that form our tradition and the unique and diverse experiences of Millennials, Gen Z, and Gen Alpha. These generations have witnessed firsthand pain caused by harm, exclusion, and mistrust that has seeped into religion. And yet, we have abundant hope and a sense of urgency to help connect faith with younger generations who are desperately seeking authenticity, belonging, and a religious and faith foundation that resonates and confirms their deepest values.

We hope this book inspires you to a call to action, a clear invitation that the church cannot (and should not) remain stagnant if it hopes to continue being a source of hope and healing in the world today. Clergy and church leaders are invited into the holy and innovative journey of creating and renewing faith communities where questions are welcomed, curiosity is encouraged, and doubt is not seen as a threat but a gateway into a deeper connection with God.

We must admit that the work ahead of us will not be easy. But it may be what is missing in our world and society today. In the holy process of grappling with our past, confronting the harm done, and committing to a time and future where we are not known for our building or traditions but for our love, the institutional church may live on. This is not a call to abandon the church, but instead, a challenge to hold on to what is life-giving and compelling to an emerging generation and to let go of what no longer points people to Jesus. This is one of those holy times and spaces to prune what may need to die so something new and beautiful may emerge. We pray for more communities and clergy to foster and co-create communities centered on love, inclusivity, unwavering commitments to justice, and a reclaiming of Jesus.

To our younger generations, Millennials, Gen Z, and Gen Alpha, we hear and support you! We see your frustration, skepticism, doubts, disappointments, and your deep longing for a real and authentic faith. We are committed to walking this journey with you, letting go of our own power and traditions to create spaces where you can encounter the divine in ways that speak to your hearts and your lives.

To our aging churches, judicatory leaders, and all who are invested in the future of the church, we have work to do! The path ahead will require courage, humility, and a willingness to change. But it is a path worth taking for the sake of the generations to come and for the future of the church we all love.

Together, we can embody a community that reflects the inclusive, loving, and transformative power of Jesus in every aspect of its life. May this be our prayer, our vision, and our future. Amen.

BONUS GUIDE

Online-Only Faith Communities

We recognize that some young adults will prefer a digital-only church experience because they were born into an online-based reality of texting, apps, and access to Wi-Fi 24/7. And for them, this is where belonging exists. When it comes to the gaming community, there are teens, youth, and emerging adults who spend most of their time with friends they have never met face to face.

When the lockdown began in March of 2020, I (Rachel) nervously went on my neighborhood Facebook Moms page and the PTA Facebook group for my kids' elementary school to figure out how to keep my kids connected to friends on online platforms. I met a mom on Facebook whose daughter was in fifth grade and wanted to play Roblox with my fifth- and seventh-grade children. Almost five years later, my kids still chat, text, and play online with this friend even though they have never met in person. And it is not just gamers or young kids on Roblox who find meaning in digital spaces.

Over a decade ago, the American Medical Association found that people with diseases can find great support, encouragement, information, and community in online support groups.[98] I had a close friend who was diagnosed with an aggressive form of cancer, and when she was unable to physically leave her house, she found a strong and empathic community online to carry her through those dark days.

Just as the Apostle Paul wrote letters to countless churches throughout the Roman Empire that were read without him physically present, we hear voices proclaiming powerful messages of hope and love that resonate with us, even when that person is not physically in our midst. You could say that the Apostle Paul was the "OG" (original) digital disciple, using other means of communicating the message so it could be more broadly shared. Without that approach to ministry, we would not have many of the books of our New Testament. Similarly, we have digital church planters in our society who are paving the way to new ways of doing ministry to reach people right where they are.

One of these digital church planters is Reverend Nathan Webb, the founding pastor of Checkpoint Church, which is physically located in North Carolina but has members worldwide. We asked him to contribute a guidebook and outline for an online ministry to help you better understand how this is presently being done effectively and fruitfully. We all have a lot to learn from Nathan as we listen to and learn from his experience doing online-only church ministry:

---

[98] https://journalofethics.ama-assn.org/article/benefits-online-health-communities/2014-04.

Digital Church

By Reverend Nathan Webb

Growing up in North Carolina, I've witnessed many a pithy southern adage. We have famous phrases and snarky comebacks. One of my favorites revolves around the weather in a state that experiences all four seasons. If someone worries that it may be too hot, cold, windy, or rainy, a lifelong North Carolinian will respond, "If you don't like the weather here in North Carolina, just wait about five minutes, and it'll change." This hyperbolic sentiment is shared by many who grew up on the East Coast of the United States.

Being raised as a digital native, I feel the sentiment is similar to this wild concept we call the Internet. As one of those under forty that this book aims to reach, I've been a part of this evolution: from dial-up to fiber, MySpace to Facebook, Twitter to X (but everyone still calls it Twitter). If you don't like the state of the Internet right now, just wait five minutes, and it'll change.

The landscape of digital interaction has evolved rapidly, and with it, the opportunities for faith formation have expanded. Understanding and effectively utilizing digital spaces is crucial for reaching young people, especially digital natives. This chapter delves into the various digital environments that can foster belonging and nurture faith, providing a comprehensive guide for faith leaders and communities.

Understanding Digital Spaces

Social media, once the epicenter of digital interaction, has transformed significantly. Platforms that were once vibrant and engaging are now rife with fatigue and negativity, leading to a phenomenon known as "doomscrolling." Users find themselves endlessly scrolling through negative content, which has resulted in a general sense of weariness and disillusionment.

At worst, encounters in these digital spaces can be exacerbated by AI users, fancy algorithms pretending to be human beings to maximize engagement online. This shift has been particularly noticeable among the spiritually curious— those seeking deeper meaning and connection. They are tired of the inauthenticity that pervades many social media spaces and yearn for genuine, meaningful interactions.

This presents both a challenge and an opportunity for faith communities. By recognizing this shift, faith leaders can strategically position themselves to offer the authenticity and community these individuals crave. But beware—try to fake it, and you'll be swiftly sniffed out.

Historically, social media platforms like Facebook, Twitter, and Instagram were heralded revolutionary tools for connection and communication. They provided unprecedented access to information and facilitated new forms of social interaction. This was especially true during the cultural mile-marker of a global pandemic that demanded we communicate nearly exclusively via these platforms. However, over time, these platforms' commercial and algorithm-driven nature has led to a saturation of content, much of which is sensationalized or negative. This saturation has contributed to a sense of burnout among users, not to mention the questionable business ethics of many of these technological behemoths, leading to increased skepticism from those focused on social justice.

This evolution necessitates a strategic pivot for faith

communities. While social media remains a powerful tool for outreach, simply being present is no longer sufficient. Content must be authentic, purposeful, and aligned with the community's values and needs to engage the under-forty demographic effectively. By refocusing, faith leaders can pivot from being content creators to effective ministers online.

Navigating the Digital Landscape

Understanding the different types of digital spaces and their unique functions is essential to effectively reaching and engaging digital natives. In this guide, I'd like to offer a framing device for social media platforms. I will do so by using an intersection of two axes: content and audience.

By the term "content," I am referring to a wide array of things an account could create online. Content includes, but is not limited to, pictures, videos, polls, reviews, comments, posts, and even platform creation itself.

By the term "audience," there is a less direct path towards a definition. Given the faith-based nature of our discussion, it is likely unhelpful to use many of the terms that the digital marketer or content creator is familiar with—demographic, engagement, etc. I am attempting to refer to a less consumer-driven body of people.

These spaces can be categorized into three major types: consumer spaces, contributor spaces, and co-creator spaces. Each serves a distinct purpose in the journey of faith formation. In my experience, the most effective methodology for ministry online is to pick just one from each space and master it. In our digital church plant, we've spent five years crafting a discipleship pathway around these three spaces and how they interact. I will offer our parallels in each section. I hope this will provide a viable path toward reaching the digital native authentically and relationally.

Consumer Spaces

Definitions & Purpose	Consumer spaces are where new members receive the content you create. These are the traditional platforms like Facebook, Instagram, and YouTube. The content in these spaces is designed to be consumed, with high competition for attention. It's where a broad audience views your messages, videos, articles, and other forms of content.
Example	Twitch is a platform with a localized culture and strong community identity. Twitch is particularly effective for live streaming, which allows real-time interaction and engagement with viewers. This platform can be leveraged for live Q&A sessions, live sermons, and interactive discussions.
Discipleship Pathway	Evangelism—this is often where individuals begin their journey. It's the starting point where people first encounter your content and community.
Challenges & Opportunities	The main challenge in consumer spaces is standing out amidst the noise. With so much content available, creating high-quality, engaging content that resonates with your audience is crucial. This requires understanding their needs, interests, and pain points. On the flip side, the opportunity lies in the vast reach of these platforms. By tapping into these spaces, you can reach a wide audience and attract new members to your community.

Contributor Spaces

Definitions & Purpose	Contributor spaces facilitate participation and engagement with content. Examples include X/Twitter, Tumblr, Reddit, and comment sections on various platforms. Here, the goal is to create engagement through interaction. These spaces are less about passive consumption and more about active involvement.
Example	YouTube comments. The comment section on YouTube can be a vibrant space for discussion, feedback, and interaction. It allows viewers to share their thoughts, ask questions, and engage with both the content and the content creator.
Discipleship Pathway	Relationship-Building—these spaces are akin to coffee dates in the digital world. They offer opportunities for deeper interaction and personal connection.
Challenges & Opportunities	The main challenge in contributor spaces is managing negative interactions and maintaining a positive environment. This requires active moderation and a proactive approach to handling conflicts and negative comments. However, the opportunity lies in building stronger relationships and a sense of community. Engaging with contributors can foster a deeper connection and encourage them to take a more active role in the community.

Co-Creator Spaces

Definitions & Purpose	Co-creator spaces are designed for collaboration and leadership development. Platforms like Discord, Slack, Mighty Networks, and Facebook Groups fall into this category. These spaces encourage members to take ownership and eventually create content themselves.
Example	Discord—Discord provides a versatile platform for real-time communication, collaboration, and community-building. It allows members to take on active roles in content creation and leadership.
Discipleship Pathway	Regular Attendance, Membership, Leadership—these are spaces for deeper engagement and community-building.
Challenges & Opportunities	The main challenge in co-creator spaces is fostering a sense of ownership and responsibility among members. This requires creating an environment where members feel valued and empowered to contribute. The opportunity lies in the potential for leadership development and community growth. By encouraging co-creation, you can build a strong, self-sustaining community.

Consumer Spaces

Consumer spaces are the platforms most people are already familiar with—Facebook, Instagram, and YouTube. These platforms are designed for content consumption, and the competition for attention is fierce. However, they also offer unparalleled reach and accessibility, making them a valuable tool for faith communities. The far reach of these platforms makes them the most effective starting place for outreach.

Facebook, for instance, has a vast user base, making it an ideal platform for reaching a broad audience. It does cater to an older demographic. Instagram, with its focus on visual content, is perfect for sharing inspirational images, stories, and short videos. It is likely to reach a younger audience than Facebook. Still, it has been around long enough that fewer Gen Z and Gen Alpha are flocking to the platform, preferring newer apps their parents are likely not present on, such as TikTok or flash-in-the-pans like BeReal. YouTube, the second largest search engine after Google, is a powerful platform for hosting longer-form content such as sermons, testimonies, and educational videos.

One is borrowing attention and tapping into existing user pipelines in these spaces. This makes it crucial to create content that stands out and meets the needs of your target demographic. To be effective, your content must be engaging but also relevant and valuable to your audience.

Consider the algorithm-driven nature of these platforms. Content that garners likes, shares, comments, and other forms of engagement is more likely to be promoted by the platform, reaching a wider audience. Creating content that resonates with your audience maximizes reach and impact.

Example: Twitch

Twitch is a platform with a strong, localized culture and identity. It allows faith communities to reach individuals through live streaming and interactive content. For example, live Q&A sessions, interactive discussions, and live sermons can be highly effective. I'm even familiar with evangelists who stream for hours on end, simply reading through the Bible with discussion between verses. The real-time interaction allows immediate feedback and engagement, creating community and connection.

Twitch also offers the advantage of fostering a sense of presence and immediacy. Unlike pre-recorded content, live streaming allows for spontaneous interaction, making the experience more engaging and authentic. Viewers can ask questions, share their thoughts, and participate in real-time discussions, creating a dynamic and interactive environment.

The secret magic of Twitch is the existing cultural pipeline. Most streaming platforms were something else at first, but Twitch, with its flaws, has been a live-streaming trendsetter since its origin. There are colloquial terms. There are inside jokes. Users share a private history. All of this has already happened (and is happening) regardless of your entity's presence on the platform.

The downside of such a strong cultural marker is that you can never fully become an insider. For churches or pastors, the space you create becomes a haven within the culture, but the culture will always move faster than the creator. The space the creator inhabits is not their own, meaning there is no upkeep. The relationships are genuine, but it also means control and boundaries are limited.

For my church plant in the space, these limitations were made evident by our inability to form our own community truly in the borrowed space. It felt like setting up camp in the middle of a local coffee shop. We could have valuable time together, but the space was never fully ours.

This experience led to language formation in our Twitch stream, the "coffee shop," where we meet new people and hand them a card with our address to find our church building. It was a stepping stone to the next phase of entering our church community. In our discipleship pathway, it takes the forefront—ideally, it is the first place we meet someone.

Consumer spaces are typically where individuals begin their faith journey. The content here should be inviting, engaging, and accessible. It should provide a clear and compelling introduction to your community and its values.

It should be noted that the space here is not for advertisement or marketing purposes. While those are important elements of effective ministry, they are no longer an effective way to invite someone into a faith community (if they ever were).

Effective evangelism in consumer spaces involves more than just sharing content. It requires creating an environment where individuals feel welcome and valued. This can involve responding to comments, engaging in discussions, and creating opportunities for further interaction. The goal is to build relationships with those of an existing culture and then create a sense of community that encourages further exploration and engagement in the next phase of the pathway.

Safety in Consumer Spaces

To create a safe and welcoming environment in consumer spaces:

- Understand the needs and preferences of your target demographic. Meet them where they are with helpful and relevant content. This requires ongoing research and engagement to align with their needs and interests.

- Availability is key. Ensure you are consistently present and responsive to engage effectively with your audience. This can involve regular posting, timely responses to comments and messages, and active participation in discussions.

- Maintaining safety also involves setting clear guidelines for behavior and interactions. This can help create a positive, respectful environment where everyone feels welcome and valued. Proactively addressing any negative behavior or interactions is important to maintain a safe and supportive community.

Contributor Spaces

Contributor spaces can be tricky to navigate. Platforms like X/Twitter, Tumblr, Reddit, and active comment sections allow for greater interaction but also come with the risk of negative engagement. To maintain a positive environment, these spaces require a proactive approach to moderation and community management.

X/Twitter, for instance, is a platform where conversations can quickly become heated and contentious. While it offers opportunities for engagement and interaction, this

154

platform also requires careful management to avoid negative interactions and maintain a positive environment.

In these spaces, you are hosting engagement within a borrowed space. The key difference between this and the consumer space is the intention behind your content. The goal is to create meaningful interactions that build community. This involves creating opportunities for members to participate, share their thoughts, and engage with the content and the community.

Effective engagement involves more than just responding to comments. It requires creating a sense of connection and community where individuals feel valued and heard. This can involve asking questions, encouraging feedback, and generating moments for further interaction and engagement.

Example: YouTube

YouTube comments can be a place for vibrant discussion and community-building. However, they require careful moderation to maintain a positive environment. Encourage constructive feedback, recognize valuable contributions, and address negative comments promptly and respectfully.

Engaging with viewers in the comment section can help build a sense of community and connection. It allows viewers to share their thoughts, ask questions, and engage with both the content and the content creator. This can foster a sense of belonging and encourage further engagement and participation.

We stumbled into this area of our discipleship pathway by accident. We originally wanted to utilize YouTube's reach as a secondary benefit for our video-essay-like sermons. We hoped our gathered community would primarily view these videos in the next space. Still, we discovered that the community forming around our consistent posting routine in the comment section was becoming viable.

It was less of a consumer relationship. The communication began to take the shape of relationship formation. This led to the next major aspect of our pathway forming around the contributions of those engaging with the content we were creating, namely sermons.

Contributor spaces are ideal for building relationships. They offer opportunities for deeper interaction and personal connection. Building relationships in contributor spaces involves creating a sense of trust and connection. This can involve sharing personal stories, asking questions, and encouraging members to share their experiences and thoughts. The goal is to create a sense of community where individuals feel valued and connected.

Most vitally, this happens over a length of time. It requires loyalty. Very few contributor spaces pop up overnight. Most are earned via trust built over many years of consistent connection. Our sermons didn't find their audience on YouTube for three years. But now it's become vital to the relationships we build online.

Safety in Contributor Spaces

To ensure safety and positive engagement in contributor spaces:

- Proactively manage and moderate interactions. Remove harmful content to maintain a respectful and supportive environment. This involves setting clear guidelines for behavior and actively enforcing them.

- Encourage constructive contributions and recognize valuable input from community members. This can involve highlighting valuable comments, thanking contributors, and creating opportunities for recognition and reward.

- Maintaining safety also involves being proactive in addressing any negative behavior or interactions. I like to frame this as "vandalism." Toxic behavior is akin to someone applying harmful graffiti to your church building or shattering a stained-glass window. My initial hesitance to delete harmful posts has now taken hold as a means of tidying up our space. Spending equal energy on keeping spaces clean as you do incentivize those contributing can be a huge boon to maximizing a positive contribution space.

Co-Creator Spaces

Churches often overlook co-creator spaces, but they hold significant potential for leadership development and community ownership. Platforms like Discord, Slack, and Mighty Networks are ideal. These spaces provide an environment where members can actively participate in content creation and leadership, fostering a sense of ownership and responsibility. Notably, these are the first places where the space you create is uniquely yours and not borrowed space on another platform. The curation of the culture is entirely dependent on the community.

These platforms allow for real-time communication and collaboration. In co-creator spaces, you create somewhat private locations where members opt in and provide an environment where members can take on active content creation and leadership roles, fostering a sense of ownership and responsibility. This kind of space involves creating opportunities for members to contribute, collaborate, and take on leadership roles.

Creating ownership involves more than just providing opportunities for participation. It requires creating an environment where members feel valued and empowered to contribute. This can involve providing support, resources, and training to help members succeed in their roles.

Example: Discord

Discord is a versatile real-time communication, collaboration, and community-building platform allowing members to take active roles in content creation and leadership. For example, members can create and lead discussion groups, organize events, and contribute to the community's development with text, audio, and video contributions.

Discord also offers the advantage of fostering a sense of presence and immediacy. Unlike asynchronous platforms, Discord allows real-time interaction and collaboration, creating a dynamic and interactive environment. Conversely, that interaction doesn't disappear, so it's also available for asynchronous consumption. This availability can foster community and connection, encouraging further engagement and participation before, during, and after community interaction.

Co-creator spaces are where members transition from simple attendance to active participation and leadership within the community. For this reason, when planting a digital church, we decided to use Discord as our space to plant our church. We fondly refer to our Discord server as "our church building." It's where we send prospective members to a digital address, so to speak.

Not only has this proven accurate for the experience of members who have joined, but it's also been a fascinatingly monastic experience. Since its launch, our Discord server has never hit zero active users. Whether at two a.m. or p.m., there are always a few dozen, if not hundreds, lurking on our server.

Whereas other spaces on the Internet have a financial relationship with sustaining consumers' time, our Discord server serves no other purpose than inviting others into co-creating culture alongside us. This unique opportunity makes this feel more like a church than many churches I've been a part of.

Safety in Co-Creator Spaces

Especially considering the final sentiment of the prior section, safety in co-creator spaces (especially monastic ones) is different from other digital venues. To maintain safety and encourage positive engagement in co-creator spaces:

- Balance moderation with freedom. Provide guidelines and support without micromanaging every interaction. This involves setting clear expectations for behavior and providing support and resources to help members succeed.

- Foster a culture of mutual respect and responsibility among members. This involves creating an environment where members feel valued and empowered to contribute, and everyone takes responsibility for maintaining a positive and supportive community.

- Much of the co-creator spaces' level of safety involves fewer rules and more proactive guidelines. At this point, trust has already begun to build. Now comes the formation of a culture. For our cultural expectations, we use the general rules of John Wesley: do good, do no harm, and (our words) strive to grow. This implies much without drudging up dozens of restrictions.

Creating and maintaining co-creator spaces requires a comprehensive approach that includes setting clear guidelines, providing resources and support, encouraging participation, fostering community, and active monitoring and moderation. Setting clear guidelines is the first step, as it establishes rules for behavior and interactions, ensuring that everyone feels welcome and valued in a positive and respectful environment.

Equally important is providing resources and support to help members succeed in their roles. This support can include offering tutorials, mentorship, and access to necessary tools and resources that empower members and facilitate their contributions. Many of these are provided by platforms such as Discord's Moderation 101 forums.

Encouraging participation is another key element. Creating opportunities for members to actively engage through events, discussion groups, or feedback sessions helps build a dynamic and interactive community. Fostering a sense of community is essential for deeper connections among members. Deeper connections can be achieved by creating social interaction opportunities, recognizing and celebrating achievements, and promoting a culture of mutual respect and support. Finally, monitoring and moderating interactions proactively ensures a positive and supportive environment. Addressing negative behavior or interactions promptly and effectively helps maintain the integrity and positivity of the space.

The Importance of Authenticity

As a final word in this section, I would be remiss not to name the most prevailing mistake that churches make online. Digital natives can quickly identify inauthenticity. Being genuine and transparent in all interactions is essential to engage this demographic effectively. This involves being honest about your intentions, values, and beliefs and then being open to feedback and dialogue.

Authenticity involves more than being honest. It requires consistency in your actions and interactions. Authenticity helps build trust and credibility with your audience, fostering a deeper sense of connection and engagement.

Building an authentic online presence involves a multifaceted approach that hinges on transparency, genuine engagement, consistency, storytelling, and openness to feedback. Transparency is foundational; being open and honest about your intentions, values, and beliefs helps establish a strong, trustworthy foundation.

Sharing your community's story and mission further solidifies this trust. Authentic engagement is crucial for meaningful interactions. Responding to comments and questions thoughtfully and participating in discussions genuinely can greatly enhance the sense of connection and community.

Additionally, sharing personal stories and experiences can humanize your online presence. These narratives foster deeper connections by allowing your audience to see the real, relatable people behind the community. Finally, being open to feedback is essential for growth and improvement. Actively seeking and responding to feedback shows that you value your audience's input and are committed to learning and evolving. This can significantly strengthen the sense of community and mutual respect.

The Lay of the Land

Reaching the digital native requires a nuanced understanding of the available digital spaces. Faith communities can create safe, engaging, and authentic environments that foster belonging and spiritual growth by effectively utilizing consumer, contributor, and co-creator spaces. The key to success lies in understanding the unique functions of these spaces, maintaining authenticity, and staying adaptable in an ever-changing digital landscape.

By embracing these strategies and principles, faith leaders can create digital spaces that attract and engage young people and foster a deep sense of belonging and community. In doing so, these approaches can help guide the next generation on their spiritual journey, providing the support, resources, and connections they need to grow and thrive in their faith.

Through intentional and thoughtful engagement in digital spaces, faith communities can create environments that are not only safe and welcoming but also dynamic and transformative. This engagement involves more than just creating content; it requires building relationships, fostering community, and creating meaningful engagement and participation opportunities.

As the digital landscape continues to evolve, faith

communities must stay informed and adaptable, continually seeking new ways to connect and engage with their audience. By doing so, faith communities can ensure that they remain relevant and effective in their mission to reach and nurture the spiritual growth of people under forty.

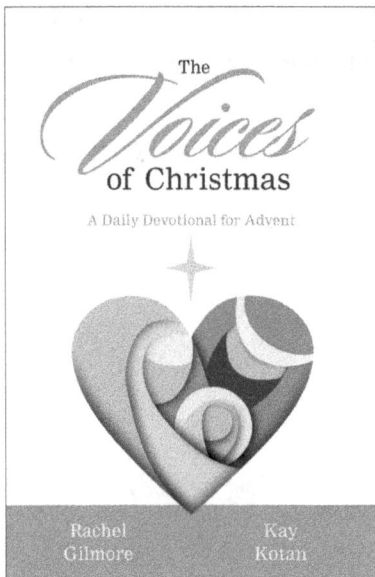

The
Voices
of Christmas

A Daily Devotional for Advent

Rachel Gilmore   Kay Kotan

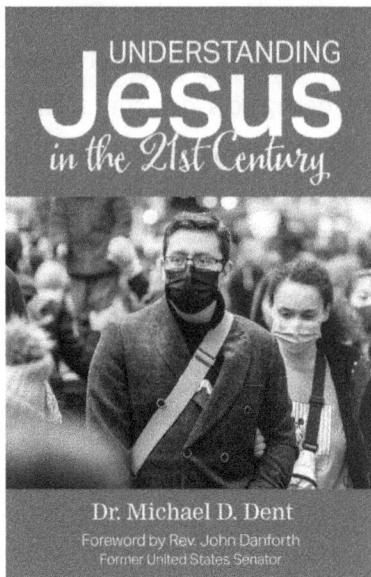

UNDERSTANDING
Jesus
in the 21st Century

Dr. Michael D. Dent

Foreword by Rev. John Danforth
Former United States Senator

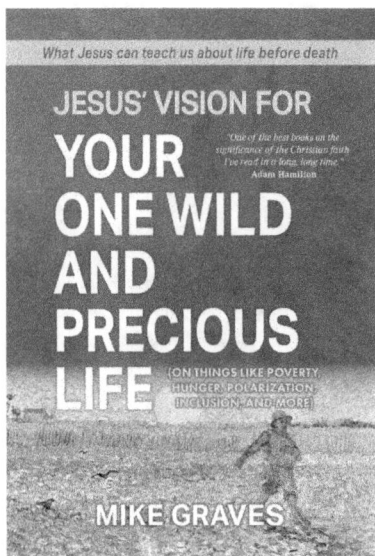

What Jesus can teach us about life before death

JESUS' VISION FOR
YOUR
ONE WILD
AND
PRECIOUS
LIFE (ON THINGS LIKE POVERTY, HUNGER, POLARIZATION, INCLUSION, AND MORE)

"One of the best books on the significance of the Christian faith I've read in a long, long time."
Adam Hamilton

MIKE GRAVES

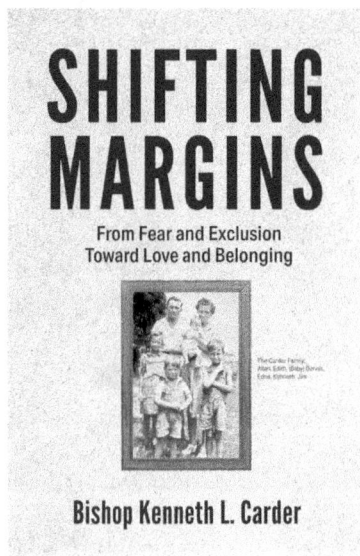

SHIFTING
MARGINS

From Fear and Exclusion
Toward Love and Belonging

Bishop Kenneth L. Carder

marketsquarebooks.com

www.ingramcontent.com/pod-product-compliance
Lightning Source LLC
Chambersburg PA
CBHW070920270326
41927CB00011B/2646